THE OFFICIAL

COOKBOOK

101 MAGICAL RECIPES FROM THE DELICIOUS DISNEY VAULT

THE OFFICIAL

Disney Parks

COOKBOOK

101 MAGICAL RECIPES FROM
THE DELICIOUS DISNEY VAULT

PAM BRANDON & THE DISNEY CHEFS

Disney
EDITIONS
Los Angeles • New York

OPPOSITE: Spring blooms circle Central Plaza, the hub within Disneyland that leads to various lands as well as the park's iconic Sleeping Beauty Castle. A sculpture of Walt Disney with Mickey Mouse, appropriately named *Partners*, is placed at its center.

EDITOR'S NOTE: Please remember that the Disney parks are constantly changing and growing, and the printed recipes you hold in your hands are our best effort at accuracy at the time of printing. If given an opportunity to update this book at a future date, we will refine and expand our materials to even better enhance your experience.

These recipes have been converted from a larger quantity in the restaurant kitchens. The flavor profile may vary from the restaurant's version.

Always use caution when handling sharp objects and hot contents, and please supervise children who are helping or nearby.

All recipes are the property of Walt Disney Parks and Resorts U.S., Inc., and may not be reproduced without express permission.

Some images shown throughout this publication do not represent current operational guidelines or health and safety measures, such as face covering and physical distancing requirements. Visit https://disneyworld.disney.go.com for important details to know before you visit.

Thank you, and enjoy!

For information address Disney Editions, 77 West 66th Street, New York, New York 10023.

Editorial Director: Wendy Lefkon
Senior Editor: Jennifer Eastwood
Assistant Editor: Lori Campos
Senior Designer: Lindsay Broderick
Managing Editor: Monica Vasquez
Production: Anne Peters and Marybeth Tregarthen

ISBN 978-1-368-09029-2
FAC-034274-22266
Printed in the United States of America
First Edition, November 2022

1 3 5 7 9 10 8 6 4 2
Visit www.disneybooks.com

THE OFFICIAL DISNEP FAN CLUB

Disney's Grand Floridian Resort & Spa, 2021

CONTENTS

INTRODUCTION
Delicious Disney

MY FIRST TRIP to the Walt Disney World Resort in the fall of 1974 was a giddy experience. We stayed at the new Golf Resort and spent all day in the Magic Kingdom, wandering through the branches of the Swiss Family Treehouse, boarding Jungle Cruise countless times to see what we missed on

the last go-around, gliding through the rooms of the Haunted Mansion, and beguiled by a talking Abe Lincoln in The Hall of Presidents. I recall it was a leisurely sort of stay, nothing rushed, no long waits for the comical Country Bear Jamboree show or our 20,000 Leagues Under the Sea submarine ride.

Recollections of a vacation often come back to food—to a special dinner eaten elbow to elbow with family and friends. I remember my first taste of the ethereal Stilton cheesecake with a vintage port at Victoria & Albert's at Disney's Grand Floridian Resort & Spa as a professional food writer, but just as fondly, I recall the old-fashioned cheeseburger and chocolate malt with my kids at Beaches & Cream Soda Shop at Disney's Beach Club Resort. Good food is part of our memories.

For Disney, it's a real balancing act to offer something for every palate, with cuisine as varied as all the guests who visit the resorts. That's why in our Official Disney Parks Cookbooks we include a bit of everything, too, with recipes that make it easy to enjoy the dishes at home. Some are fuss-free; others take a little time. Some are classics; others are new adventures.

OPPOSITE: A view down Main Street, U.S.A. in 1974, the year of Pam's first trip to the Magic Kingdom.

ABOVE: Within the Swiss Family Treehouse in the Magic Kingdom, the main dining table—and nearby kitchen area—is the heart of the home, even when that home is a fantastical tree house.

I wrote the first "official Disney parks cookbook" in partnership with the Disney chefs and the Disney Parks Food & Beverage team nearly twenty-five years ago. *Cooking with Mickey and the Disney Chefs of Walt Disney World Resort* (Hyperion, 1998) was the first-of-its-kind cookbook and a special collaboration that has led to an entire specialty industry of theme park culinary recipes. The aim of that first very first cookbook—plus, the near baker's dozen to follow—was to present favorite recipes that are both "home-cook-friendly" and true to the flavors and processes thoughtfully developed at Disney. Though the Disney chefs must serve hundreds, all of the official recipes have been adapted to family-size servings and tested for actual home use. Over the years, I've enjoyed working with the talented and amiable Disney chefs, sifting through hundreds of their dishes to choose the very best, downsizing recipes, and testing them to ensure they will work well in a home kitchen.

What you hold in your hand is 101 recipes from this now quite vast collection of official Disney Parks recipes. The collection is a best of the best from coast to coast. Knowing how the menus at the Disney resorts and aboard the cruise ships so often change with the seasons and the trends, I have complete appreciation for the recipes that have incredible staying power, like Walt's Chili and Beans, the Monte Cristo Sandwich, and, of course, DOLE Whip®. Likewise, no cookbook of favorites would be complete without some dishes and restaurants that are gone, but nonetheless warmly remembered. Some recipes inside are from the award-winning restaurants, like Napa Rose at Disney's Grand Californian Hotel & Spa at the Disneyland Resort or Sanaa at Disney's Animal Kingdom Villas—Kidani Village at the Walt

Disney World Resort. Others more recently entered the Disney dining scene, like decadent drinks from Remy aboard the Disney Cruise Line ships or Oga's Cantina at *Star Wars*: Galaxy's Edge. There's an abundance of tastes and flavors to try, and the choices are seemingly endless.

The volume is organized to reflect the best practices of Disney cookbook making. Because memories are so often tied to physical places, the chapters are aligned by particular theme parks and resorts. And since planning a home meal requires a home chef to be well organized, each chapter is set up to reflect the meal type: "Starters," "Mains and Sides," and "Sweet Endings and Desserts." And for a little extra Disney magic, there's an ID badge and brief introduction to give you more details on each recipe or location where it originated—from "kid-friendly" notices to fun facts.

We hope this exciting collection helps you re-create cherished vacation memories at home—and most of all, we invite you back to our table, to experience the delightful and delicious foods of Disney. May you share these great meals with great friends and family for many years to come.

—Pam Brandon

April 2022

Sleeping Beauty Castle, 2019

CHAPTER ONE
Disneyland

WALT'S CHILI AND BEANS

STARTERS

This was Walt Disney's favorite meal. The orginal Disneyland version of the recipe appeared seasonally through the years at restaurants such as Plaza Inn and River Belle Terrace. Over time, the ingredients evolved, too, with past versions including dried thyme and paprika. This is the current version and mainstay at Carnation Café on Main Street, U.S.A.

SERVES 6-8　　　　　　**A DISNEY CLASSIC**

CHILI

¼ cup olive oil, divided

¾ pound beef stew meat

1 small onion, diced

1 medium green pepper, diced

4 cloves garlic, minced

1 pound ground beef

1 tablespoon ground cumin

1 ½ tablespoons chili powder

1 tablespoon onion powder

¾ teaspoon cayenne pepper

3 tablespoons tomato paste

2 plum tomatoes, diced

1 (28-ounce) can diced tomatoes

2 tablespoons beef base

1 ½ cups water

1 (14.5-ounce) can pinto beans, rinsed and drained

Coarse salt, to taste

FOR CHILI

1. Heat 2 tablespoons of the oil in large Dutch oven, over medium heat for 5 minutes. Add stew meat and sauté for 10 minutes, until meat is browned on all sides. Remove stew meat from pan and set aside.

2. Add the remaining 2 tablespoons of oil to pan, heat for 3 minutes over medium heat.

3. Add onions and green pepper. Sauté 8 to 10 minutes, until soft. Add garlic and sauté one minute longer, until garlic is fragrant.

4. Add ground beef. Cook, stirring occasionally to break up large chunks of beef, for 10 to 12 minutes, until beef is no longer pink. Drain excess fat.

5. Return stew meat to the Dutch oven with ground beef mixture. Add ground cumin, chili powder, onion powder, cayenne pepper, tomato paste, diced plum tomatoes, diced can tomatoes, beef base, and water.

6 Bring chili to a simmer. Cover and simmer over low heat for 3 hours, until stew meat is tender.

7 Add pinto beans. Simmer for 10 minutes, until beans are warm.

8 Season with salt, as needed.

TO SERVE

Garnish with sour cream, shredded cheddar cheese, and diced tomatoes.

GARNISH

½ cup sour cream

1 cup shredded cheddar cheese

2 small tomatoes, diced

LOADED BAKED POTATO SOUP

For cooking this rich and creamy soup, soak diced potatoes in cold water until ready to use to keep them from turning brown. To make bacon easier to chop, lightly freeze.

SERVES 6   **LEFT THE MENU BUT NOT FORGOTTEN**

1 In a 6- to 8-quart stockpot over medium heat, carefully fry bacon until crisp.

2 Remove bacon and drain on paper towels (reserve half for garnish). In the bacon fat, cook onions, carrots, and celery until the onions are translucent. Add potatoes and cook for 4 minutes, stirring occasionally.

3 Sprinkle in flour and stir constantly over low heat about 5 to 7 minutes until mixture has thickened slightly. Add stock and half of bacon. Season with salt and pepper.

4 Over medium-high heat, bring the soup to a simmer and cook for 25 minutes, or until the potatoes are soft. Mash some of the potatoes for thicker, creamier texture. Add cream and simmer for 5 minutes.

5 Adjust thickness by adding water or stock. Soup should have a creamy consistency.

6 Season to taste, and garnish with toppings if desired.

1 pound bacon, roughly chopped

1 medium yellow onion, diced

1 large carrot, peeled and diced

¾ cup diced celery

4 large russet potatoes, peeled and diced

4 medium red potatoes, diced

¼ cup flour

2 cups chicken or vegetable stock

coarse salt, to taste

freshly ground pepper, to taste

4 cups heavy cream

OPTIONAL GARNISHES

chopped chives

bacon bits

sour cream

shredded cheeses, cheddar and Monterey Jack preferred

POMMES FRITES WITH CAJUN RÉMOULADE

Known for New Orleans–style dishes, Cafe Orleans opened in New Orleans Square in 1972 and replaced the Creole Cafe (1966–1972). These spicy "fried potatoes" seem right at home.

SERVES 4

SAVORY BITES

FOR CAJUN RÉMOULADE

1 Mix together all ingredients except salt and pepper in a medium mixing bowl.

2 Season to taste; refrigerate until ready to use.

FOR POMMES FRITES

1 Mix together garlic, Cajun seasoning, Parmesan cheese, parsley, and salt in a large mixing bowl; set aside.

2 Carefully heat oil in a large heavy pot over high heat to 375°F. Check the heat by carefully dipping a french fry in the oil; the oil is hot enough if it immediately sizzles.

3 With caution, fry the french fries in batches, being careful not to crowd, cooking 4 to 5 minutes or until crisp and golden brown.

4 Transfer to paper towels to drain, then lightly toss in the cheese mixture. Serve hot with Cajun rémoulade.

CAJUN RÉMOULADE

1 cup Thousand Island dressing

½ cup mayonnaise

1 teaspoon finely chopped garlic

¼ teaspoon lemon juice

½ teaspoon Dijon-style mustard

1 pinch paprika

1 teaspoon Worcestershire sauce

½ teaspoon Cajun seasoning

coarse salt, to taste

freshly ground white pepper, to taste

POMMES FRITES

1 tablespoon finely chopped garlic

½ teaspoon Cajun seasoning

⅓ cup grated Parmesan cheese

1 teaspoon chopped fresh parsley

½ teaspoon coarse salt

8 cups vegetable oil

16 ounces frozen french fries

BATUUAN RONTO WRAP

For those times when you want to let a droid do the cooking—but don't have a podracer to get to Black Spire Outpost—you can make Batuuan Ronto Wraps at home. Soon you'll be eating like a citizen of Batuu.

SERVES 8

A DISNEY CLASSIC

FOR ROASTED PORK SHOULDER

1. Preheat oven to 300°F. Pat pork dry with paper towel. Rub with canola oil and season with salt and pepper.

2. Place seasoned pork butt on the rack of a roasting pan and cook for 3 hours, until pork is 160°F.

3. Cool for at least 15 minutes, then carve to ⅛-inch-thick slices.

FOR RONTO WRAP SLAW

1. Combine apple cider vinegar, sambal, sugar, canola oil, dried parsley, salt, and pepper in a large mixing bowl.

2. Add matchstick carrots and shredded cabbage and toss until combined.

3. Refrigerate until ready to serve.

FOR PEPPERCORN SAUCE

1. Combine all ingredients in a large mixing bowl.

2. Refrigerate until ready to serve.

ROASTED PORK SHOULDER

2 pounds pork butt

2 tablespoons canola oil

2 tablespoons coarse salt

½ teaspoon black pepper

RONTO WRAP SLAW

⅓ cup apple cider vinegar

2½ tablespoons sambal

2 tablespoons sugar

2 tablespoons canola oil

1 tablespoon dried parsley

1 teaspoon coarse salt

1 teaspoon black pepper

1 cup matchstick carrots

3 cups shredded cabbage

PEPPERCORN SAUCE

1 cup mayonnaise

1 tablespoon lime juice

1 tablespoon apple cider vinegar

1 teaspoon ground sumac

½ tablespoon coarse salt

¼ teaspoon ground coriander

⅛ teaspoon Szechuan peppercorns

FOR GRILLED OR TOASTED PITA BREAD

1 Preheat grill or sauté pan over medium heat. Brush pan or grill with oil.

2 Toast bread for 1 minute on each side, until golden brown. Keep warm until ready to serve.

FOR GRILLED SAUSAGES

1 Preheat grill pan over medium heat for 5 minutes. Grill sausages for 5 to 7 minutes, turning once, until internal temperature reaches 160°F.

2 Add reserved pork slices to pan and cook until golden brown on both sides.

3 Keep warm until ready to serve.

TO SERVE

Place 2 slices of pork roast on each piece of pita bread. Place one grilled sausage on top. Top each wrap with ½ cup of Ronto Wrap Slaw and drizzle with Peppercorn Sauce.

GRILLED OR TOASTED PITA BREAD

1 tablespoon canola oil

8 pita flatbreads

GRILLED SAUSAGES

8 (4-ounce) smoked sausages

SOUTH SEAS ISLAND DELIGHT

Today the cross street of Main Street, U.S.A., known as West Center Street, is filled with outdoor seating for Carnation Café, which extends inside and rounds the corner to begin the west side's northern block. Next to it is the Gibson Girl Ice Cream Parlor, followed by the Penny Arcade, Candy Palace, and the Refreshment Corner.

In 1955, this block began with Carnation Ice Cream Parlor and Puffin Bakery next to the Penny Arcade. Sunkist Citrus House occupied the bakery space (1960–1989) until reopening as the Blue Ribbon Bakery in 1990. The current configuration began in 1997 along with the opening of Carnation Café. The now iconic patio restaurant expanded in 2012 when the bakery left the block.

2 scoops pineapple sherbet

¼ cup strawberry topping

2 tablespoons shredded coconut

whipped cream, for garnish

maraschino cherry, for garnish

SERVES 1

MOCKTAIL

1 Place sherbet, strawberry topping, and coconut in a blender and process until smooth.

2 Pour into a tall fountain glass and garnish with whipped cream and cherry.

LEMON SODA FLOAT

Here's a fresh and creamy dessert drink the whole family can enjoy!

SERVES 4

MOCKTAIL

1 pint vanilla ice cream

1 (2-liter) bottle lemon-lime soda

whipped cream, for garnish

maraschino cherry, for garnish

1 Divide ice cream among 4 glasses. Pour 2 cups lemon-lime soda over ice cream in each glass.

2 Top with whipped cream and cherry, if desired.

CARNATION CAFÉ · MAIN STREET, U.S.A.

RAINBOW SPRINKLE WHOOPIE PIES

What could be more fun than these Rainbow Sprinkle Whoopie Pies? A childhood treat made with cocoa-rich cookies and fluffy white filling, this confection is a popular on-the-go snack at Jolly Holiday Bakery Cafe. You can even cheat and just use marshmallow fluff in the middle.

MAKES 18–24 PIES

GREAT FOR KIDS

CHOCOLATE WHOOPIE PIES

2 cups all-purpose flour

½ cup cocoa powder

1 cup vegetable shortening

1 cup packed brown sugar

1 teaspoon baking soda

½ teaspoon salt

1 egg

1 teaspoon vanilla extract

1 cup milk

WHITE CHOCOLATE MOUSSE

½ cup white chocolate chips

¼ teaspoon powdered gelatin

2 tablespoons water

2 eggs

1 ½ tablespoons sugar

¾ cup heavy cream

½ cup crushed chocolate sandwich cookies

Rainbow sprinkles, for garnish

FOR CHOCOLATE WHOOPIE PIES

1. Preheat oven to 350°F. Line 2 baking sheets with parchment paper; set aside.

2. Sift together flour and cocoa powder into a large bowl; set aside.

3. Beat together shortening, brown sugar, baking soda, and salt until creamy. Blend in egg and vanilla extract.

4. Alternately add milk and flour mixture, mixing until just combined.

5. Drop batter by the heaping tablespoonful onto prepared baking sheets. Bake 5 to 8 minutes, or until cookies are puffed and set.

6. Remove from oven and cool completely.

FOR WHITE CHOCOLATE MOUSSE

1. Place white chocolate chips in a heatproof bowl set over a small saucepan of simmering water, making sure bottom of bowl does not touch water. Melt, stirring frequently. Remove from heat and set aside until cooled slightly.

2 Sprinkle gelatin over water in a small bowl and set aside for 5 minutes. Microwave 10 seconds, stirring gelatin until melted.

3 Beat eggs and sugar together in the bowl of an electric mixer until pale yellow.

4 Add gelatin mixture to egg mixture; beat well to combine. Add melted white chocolate, beating well to combine.

5 Whip heavy cream to soft peaks in a separate large bowl, then gently fold whipped cream into white chocolate mixture. Gently fold in crushed chocolate sandwich cookies.

TO SERVE

1 Spread about 2 generous tablespoons of filling onto flat sides of half of cookies; top with other half of cookies.

2 Place rainbow sprinkles on a large flat plate. Gently roll each whoopie pie in sprinkles so that sprinkles adhere to filling.

FROZEN PINEAPPLE TREAT INSPIRED BY DOLE WHIP®

In 1976, Dole Packaged Foods became the sponsor of Walt Disney's Enchanted Tiki Room in Disneyland. DOLE Whip® is now an iconic frozen treat and a fan favorite for so many Disney theme park guests.

SERVES 4

A DISNEY CLASSIC

½ to ¾ cup pineapple juice, divided

2 cups frozen pineapple chunks

1 cup dairy-free vanilla ice cream

1 Place ½ cup pineapple juice, frozen pineapple, and dairy-free vanilla ice cream in blender and blend until smooth. Do not over-blend. If the mixture is too thick, add 2 tablespoons of pineapple juice at a time.

2 Scoop into bowls and serve immediately.

MICKEY MOUSE BEIGNETS

These crisp beignets are best when warm, so don't delay eating them. If you don't have a Mickey Mouse-shaped cutter, simply cut the dough into squares—they taste just as scrumptious.

MAKES 10 LARGE MICKEY MOUSE-SHAPED FRITTERS OR 2 DOZEN SMALL FRITTERS

A DISNEY CLASSIC

½ teaspoon dry yeast

¼ cup warm water (105°F)

¼ cup sugar

2 tablespoons vegetable shortening

½ teaspoon salt

½ cup heavy cream

1 egg

4 cups all-purpose flour

½ cup boiling water

vegetable oil for frying

powdered sugar

1 Sprinkle yeast over warm water in a small bowl, stirring to dissolve. Let stand for 5 minutes.

2 Combine sugar, shortening, salt, heavy cream, egg, flour, and boiling water in a large bowl; stir in yeast mixture.

3 With dough hook attachment of an electric mixer on medium speed, mix the dough just until combined and smooth. Let dough rest for 30 minutes.

4 Roll to ¼-inch thickness and cut individual beignets with a Mickey Mouse-shaped cutter or cut into 2½- to 3-inch squares. Cover with a towel and let dough rise until doubled in size in a warm, draft-free area, about 1 to 1½ hours.

5 Very carefully heat 3 inches of vegetable oil to 350°F in a deep, heavy pot over medium-high heat. With caution, fry beignets until golden brown, about 2 to 3 minutes, turning as soon as they brown on one side.

6 Remove with tongs and place on paper towels to drain. Dust warm beignets with powdered sugar and serve immediately.

TRES LECHES CAKE

SWEET ENDINGS AND DESSERTS

Literally "cake of three milks," Tres Leches is made with whole milk, sweetened condensed milk, and heavy cream. Rancho del Zocalo was known to serve a traditional Mexican version with a whipped cream topping, but meringue is also an option, as pictured here.

MAKES 1 (9×13) CAKE   **LEFT THE MENU BUT NOT FORGOTTEN**

FOR CAKE

1 Preheat oven to 325°F. Lightly grease a 9×13×2-inch cake pan.

2 Whisk together flour, baking powder, and salt in a small mixing bowl. Set aside.

3 Combine oil, sugar, and vanilla extract in a large mixing bowl. Add the eggs one at a time and mix thoroughly. Stir in ½ cup of milk and gently fold in the flour mixture until just combined.

4 Pour batter into cake pan and bake for 30 minutes or until it feels firm and an inserted toothpick comes out clean. Let cake cool to room temperature.

5 Pierce cake with a fork 30 to 40 times. Whisk together remaining ¾ cup of milk, sweetened condensed milk, 1 cup heavy cream and rum (optional). Slowly pour over cooked cake. Refrigerate for at least 1 hour.

FOR WHIPPED CREAM TOPPING

Combine ingredients in a medium bowl. With an electric mixer on medium-high speed, beat mixture until peaks form. Spread over top of cake.

CAKE

1¼ cups cake or pastry flour

1 teaspoon baking powder

⅛ teaspoon salt

⅓ cup canola oil

1 cup sugar

1 teaspoon vanilla extract

5 large eggs

1¼ cups whole milk, divided

1 cup sweetened condensed milk

1 cup heavy cream

1 tablespoon rum, optional

WHIPPED CREAM TOPPING

¾ cup heavy cream

1 teaspoon vanilla

1 tablespoon sugar

FOR MERINGUE, ALTERNATIVE TOPPING OPTION

1 In a medium glass or stainless steel bowl, beat egg whites with an electric mixer on high speed until soft peaks form. With mixer running, add sugar in a steady stream, beating until stiff peaks form.

2 Spread over top of cake. Broil 1 to 2 minutes, until meringue is golden brown. (A scant dusting of powdered sugar will help meringue nicely brown and add crunch). Note the pictured dessert has this topping.

MERINGUE, ALTERNATIVE TOPPING OPTION

4 egg whites

1 cup sugar

Guardians of the Galaxy - Mission: BREAKOUT!, 2017

CHAPTER TWO
Disney California Adventure

HOLIDAY HAM SLIDER WITH PINEAPPLE CHERRY JAM

STARTERS

Building on the concept of Holidays around the World at EPCOT, Disney California Adventure debuted Disney Festival of Holidays in 2016. The Disney chefs have fun creating indulgent small bites for the Festival Food Marketplaces with whimsical names such as "Joy to the Sauce," "Making Spirits Bright," and "Winter Sinderland." Global music fills the air, and it all culminates in January with a jubilant celebration of Three Kings' Day.

MAKES 8 SLIDERS   **FESTIVAL FAVORITE TO REMEMBER**

PINEAPPLE CHERRY JAM

2 tablespoons butter

1 white onion, diced

1 fresh pineapple, cored and diced

½ cup apple cider vinegar

¼ cup sugar

¼ cup dried cherries

2 tablespoons yellow mustard

Coarse salt, to taste

FOR PINEAPPLE CHERRY JAM

1. Melt butter in medium saucepan. Add onion and cook for 5 minutes, or until translucent.

2. Add pineapple, vinegar, and sugar; cook on low heat for 45 minutes, until vinegar and pineapple juices are reduced and pineapple begins to break down.

3. Stir in cherries and mustard; season with salt.

4. Refrigerate until ready to serve.

FOR HAM SLIDER

1 Preheat griddle or skillet over medium heat. Cut brioche buns in half and spread butter on cut side. Toast on hot griddle for 1 minute, or until golden brown.

2 Heat a sauté pan over medium heat and warm ham.

3 Evenly divide ham on warm brioche buns and top with jam.

COOK'S NOTE: Refrigerate any leftover jam—it's delicious spread on warm buttered toast.

HAM SLIDER

8 brioche buns

2 tablespoons softened butter

1 ½ pounds applewood smoked ham, sliced medium thickness

GRILLED ASPARAGUS CAESAR SALAD

The grassy notes and acidity of a sauvignon blanc make a delicious paring with this dish featured at the Eat Your Greens Marketplace stand at Disney California Adventure Food & Wine Festival.

As for anchovy fillets versus anchovy paste? If you don't want to buy a can of anchovies to use half a fillet, buy a tube of anchovy paste, because it will keep in your fridge for at least a year. The potent, salty paste adds a savory umami to all sorts of dishes, like stews, soups, and pasta sauces.

SERVES 4-6   **FESTIVAL FAVORITE TO REMEMBER**

CAESAR DRESSING

2 cloves garlic, chopped

½ teaspoon Dijon mustard

1 egg yolk

2 teaspoons red wine vinegar

½ anchovy fillet or ¼ teaspoon anchovy paste

¼ teaspoon coarsely ground black pepper

½ teaspoon coarse salt

1 tablespoon lemon juice

¼ cup freshly grated Parmesan cheese

½ cup canola oil

FOR CAESAR DRESSING

1 Combine all ingredients except canola oil in a small bowl.

2 Blend with an immersion blender until smooth.

3 Slowly add oil while blending, and blend until thick and smooth. Refrigerate until ready to serve.

FOR GRILLED ASPARAGUS

1 Place asparagus in large bowl. Add remaining ingredients, mixing to combine.

2 Heat grill pan over medium heat until hot. Grill asparagus just until tender and slightly charred, about 5 minutes.

3 Keep warm until ready to serve.

TO SERVE

Place asparagus on plates. Drizzle with Caesar dressing and top with croutons and Parmesan cheese.

GRILLED ASPARAGUS

30 medium asparagus spears (about 1 pound), trimmed

1 tablespoon canola oil

1 teaspoon coarse salt

1 shallot, peeled and chopped

4 cloves garlic, chopped

SALAD

1 cup garlic croutons

Parmesan curls, for garnish

WATERMELON LEMONADE

With this bright beverage, celebrate the bounty of the Golden State at the Disney California Adventure Food & Wine Festival, where flavors are inspired by the abundant harvest of the state's rich farmland and vineyards. This fruity fusion was served at the 2018 festival.

SERVES 1   **FESTIVAL FAVORITE TO REMEMBER**

CHILI-LIME SEASONING

1 tablespoon chipotle or chili powder

1 teaspoon lime zest

cayenne, to taste

coriander, to taste

cumin, to taste

salt, to taste

sugar, to taste

WATERMELON LEMONADE

equal parts chili-lime seasoning and habanero sugar, for rim of glass

lemon juice, for rim of glass

7 ounces lemonade

1 ounce watermelon syrup

Lemon, watermelon slices, for garnish

FOR CHILI-LIME SEASONING

Mix ingredients together.

FOR WATERMELON LEMONADE

1 Mix together chili-lime seasoning and habanero sugar.

2 Dip rim of glass in lemon juice, then chili-lime-sugar mix.

3 Combine lemonade and watermelon syrup in shaker with ice.

4 Strain into prepared glass and add ice.

5 Garnish with lemon and watermelon slices.

BEET KOMBUCHA SANGRIA

You could make both the sangria and the kombucha from scratch, but this recipe is more about a quick, easy conversation starter. A fermented drink made with tea, sugar, bacteria, and yeast, kombucha has a slight effervescence and sweet-tart flavor, a tasty blend with sangria. If you can't find beet, another flavor would work fine.

5 ounces favorite white sangria

3 ounces beet kombucha

2 to 4 fresh blackberries

SERVES 1   **FESTIVAL FAVORITE TO REMEMBER**

1 Combine sangria and kombucha in a glass. Gently stir and add ice.

2 Garnish with blackberries, if desired.

SHRIMP BOIL TACOS WITH ANDOUILLE SAUSAGE, FRESH CORN

This dish was featured at the On the Cob Marketplace stand at Disney California Adventure Food & Wine Festival. A Riesling with a hint of sweetness will cool the spiciness of the andouille sausage.

SERVES 4-6   **FESTIVAL FAVORITE TO REMEMBER**

FOR SHRIMP BOIL TACO FILLING

1. Peel and devein shrimp. Remove tails and cut shrimp into bite-size pieces.

2. Melt butter in large skillet over medium heat. Add Old Bay, Cajun seasoning, paprika, cayenne, and garlic. Cook for 1 to 2 minutes, or until garlic and spices are fragrant. Add shrimp and cook 3 to 4 minutes, or until pink and opaque.

3. Add sausage and corn and cook for 5 minutes, until heated through.

4. Keep warm until ready to serve.

TO SERVE

1. Carefully heat oil in large skillet until shimmering and add tortillas in batches. Cook for a few seconds on each side, until soft and warm. Drain on paper towels.

2. Top fried tortillas with shrimp mixture. Garnish with chopped cilantro.

3. Serve with lime wedges.

SHRIMP BOIL TACO FILLING

1 ½ pounds medium shrimp

2 sticks unsalted butter

2 tablespoons Old Bay seasoning

1 tablespoon Cajun seasoning

1 ½ teaspoons paprika

½ teaspoon cayenne pepper

4 garlic cloves, chopped

2 links andouille sausage, diced

kernels from 4 ears fresh corn

TACOS

1 tablespoon canola oil

12 (4-inch) blue or yellow corn tortillas

1 bunch cilantro, chopped

2 limes, cut into quarters

MONTE CRISTO

As a longtime Disneyland favorite that's well-known in New Orleans Square in Disneyland, the Monte Cristo—for a time—also made its way to Grizzly Peak in Disney California Adventure.

MAKES 4 SANDWICHES　　　**A DISNEY CLASSIC**

1 egg

1¾ cups plus 2 tablespoons water

1¾ cups all-purpose flour

¼ teaspoon salt

1 teaspoon baking powder

8 slices egg bread (challah works well), sliced ½ inch thick

8 thin slices ham

8 thin slices turkey

8 thin slices Swiss cheese

3 cups canola oil

Confectioners' sugar

Blackberry preserves

1　Line cookie sheet with paper towels; set aside.

2　Whisk the egg and water together in a mixing bowl. Add flour, salt, and baking powder and whisk thoroughly for 2 to 3 minutes, or until smooth, scraping side of bowl.

3　On one slice of bread, arrange 2 slices of ham, turkey, and cheese, covering the bread evenly. Place another slice of bread on top and slice each sandwich in half diagonally.

4　Carefully heat oil to between 365°F and 375°F in a 10-inch pan. Do not let the oil reach a higher temperature than this; if the oil starts to smoke, turn the heat down. Dip half of the sandwich into the batter, allowing excess to drain, and very carefully place into the oil.

5　Repeat with the other sandwich half. Cook 3 minutes on each side, or until golden brown. Place the cooked sandwich on the prepared cookie sheet in a warm oven until ready to serve. Repeat with the other three sandwiches. Cook one at a time, and allow the oil to reach the desired temperature between each.

6　Sprinkle with confectioners' sugar, and serve with blackberry preserves on the side.

OPPOSITE, BOTTOM: The iconic mountain towering over the themed area of Grizzly Peak.

WHITE HOT CHOCOLATE WITH CINNAMON MARSHMALLOWS

This sweet drink shines bright at the joyful Disney Festival of Holidays, which honors special winter celebrations such as Christmas, Hanukkah, Diwali, Kwanzaa, and Three Kings' Day.

SERVES 1　　　　**FESTIVAL FAVORITE TO REMEMBER**

CINNAMON MARSHMALLOWS

Makes 24

¾ ounce (3 packets) unflavored gelatin

1 cup water, divided

2 cups sugar

⅓ cup light corn syrup

1 pinch salt

½ tablespoon cinnamon extract

⅛ teaspoon ground cinnamon

½ cup cornstarch

½ cup powdered sugar

FOR CINNAMON MARSHMALLOWS

1 Spray a 9×13-inch pan with nonstick spray.

2 Mix gelatin with ½ cup of water in bowl of electric mixer. Set aside.

3 In medium saucepan, mix together remaining ½ cup of water, sugar, and corn syrup.

4 Cook over medium heat for 12 to 15 minutes, until mixture reaches 240°F. Remove from heat and rest for 1 minute, until temperature reaches 230°F. Pour sugar mixture into gelatin and water.

5 Whip on medium speed for 2 minutes, or until mixture begins to thicken. Add salt. Continue to whip for 8 to 10 minutes, until mixture doubles in size.

6 Add cinnamon extract. Whip for 1 minute.

7 Spray a spatula with nonstick cooking spray. Pour marshmallow mixture into prepared 9×13-inch pan. Smooth using spatula. Marshmallow will be very sticky.

8 Sprinkle cinnamon on top of marshmallows. Rest for 4 hours, or until set.

9 Combine cornstarch and powdered sugar in a small bowl.

10 Once marshmallow mixture is set, lightly brush a knife with oil, then cut into 24 squares. Roll in cornstarch and powdered sugar mixture. Store in airtight container.

FOR WHITE HOT CHOCOLATE

1 Stir together milk, vanilla, and white chocolate chips in a saucepan. Bring to a simmer over medium-low heat, stirring occasionally.

2 Serve hot, topped with cinnamon marshmallows.

WHITE HOT CHOCOLATE

1 cup milk

1 drop vanilla extract

¼ cup white chocolate chips

WHITE CHOCOLATE PEPPERMINT BAR

On the second floor of a detailed reproduction of the iconic Carthay Circle Theatre, this pretty restaurant reflects the romance and glamour of Hollywood's Golden Age—though the menu is thoroughly modern. This popular dessert marries dark chocolate crust and a creamy frozen peppermint filling with fanciful meringues for a light, crunchy finish.

SERVES 12 **GREAT FOR KIDS**

FOR CHOCOLATE COOKIE CRUST

1 Place cookies in a large resealable plastic bag, pressing out air. Crush cookies into fine crumbs with a rolling pin.

2 Add melted butter and salt, and squeeze bag to combine.

3 Press into bottom of 9x13-inch baking dish. Set aside.

FOR WHITE CHOCOLATE PEPPERMINT FILLING

1 Dissolve gelatin in cold water for 5 to 10 minutes.

2 Place white chocolate chips in a double boiler or heatproof bowl placed over a pan of simmering water. Stir until chocolate is melted. Set aside and keep warm.

3 Combine milk and salt in a small saucepan and bring to boil over medium heat. Remove from heat and stir in gelatin. Immediately pour over melted white chocolate, stirring until combined. Stir in peppermint extract and set aside.

CHOCOLATE COOKIE CRUST

24 chocolate sandwich cookies

4 tablespoons butter, melted

½ teaspoon salt

WHITE CHOCOLATE PEPPERMINT FILLING

1 tablespoon powdered gelatin

¼ cup cold water

1 ½ pounds white chocolate chips

1 ¼ cups milk

½ teaspoon coarse salt

1 teaspoon peppermint extract

1 ½ cups heavy cream

4 Whip heavy cream using electric mixer until medium-stiff peaks form.

5 Gently fold whipped cream into white chocolate peppermint mixture.

6 Pour over chocolate cookie crust. Freeze for at least 3 hours, up to 2 days.

FOR PEPPERMINT MERINGUE KISSES

1 Preheat oven to 175°F. Place egg whites and cream of tartar in bowl of electric mixer. Beat on high speed until stiff peaks form. Add sugar, ¼ cup at a time, whipping for 30 seconds after each addition.

2 Add peppermint extract and beat for 30 seconds more.

3 Place large star tip on pastry bag. Using a clean, thin paintbrush or the tip of a knife, draw stripes of red gel food coloring inside pastry tip. Fill bag with meringue.

4 Pipe meringue into forty-eight 1-inch cookies on a parchment-lined baking sheet. Gently pull up top of piping bag and tip to create a peak on top of each cookie.

5 Bake for 3 hours or until cookies harden. Remove from oven, cool, and store in airtight container.

TO SERVE

Cut frozen white chocolate peppermint bars into 12 rectangles. Place 1 bar and 4 meringue cookies on each plate.

PEPPERMINT MERINGUE KISSES

3 egg whites

¼ teaspoon cream of tartar

¾ cup sugar

¼ teaspoon peppermint extract

Red gel food coloring

WATSONVILLE STRAWBERRY PIE TARTS

SWEET ENDINGS AND DESSERTS

From the Strawberry Patch Marketplace at the Disney California Adventure Food & Wine Festival, this treat is a fresh delight.

MAKES 16 TARTS **FESTIVAL FAVORITE TO REMEMBER**

PASTRY CREAM

½ whole vanilla bean

2 cups whole milk

¼ cup plus ⅓ cup sugar

2 egg yolks

1 egg

¼ cup cornstarch

2 tablespoons butter

1 teaspoon vanilla extract

FOR PASTRY CREAM

1 Cut vanilla bean in half lengthwise; scrape out seeds.

2 Heat vanilla bean seeds, vanilla bean shell, milk, and ¼ cup sugar in medium pot over medium heat and bring almost to a boil.

3 Whisk egg yolks, whole egg, and ⅓ cup sugar and cornstarch in medium bowl until combined.

4 Whisk ½ cup of hot milk mixture into egg mixture; whisk into remaining hot milk mixture.

5 Cook over medium-low heat, stirring constantly until thickened.

6 Remove from heat and discard vanilla bean shell.

7 Stir in butter and vanilla extract.

8 Cover with plastic wrap directly on cream and refrigerate until cool.

FOR TARTS

1   Bake tart shells according to package directions until golden brown and fully baked. Cool completely.

2   Lightly brush inside of each shell with white coating chocolate.

3   Once white chocolate sets, pipe or scoop pastry cream into shells to three-quarters full.

4   Slice half of strawberries in 4 slices lengthwise. Place 1 whole strawberry (tip pointed up) in center and lean 4 strawberry quarters (tips pointed up) against the whole strawberry to create a tower.

5   Warm strawberry glaze and lightly brush onto each tart.

6   Gently press croquant around edge of each pie (optional).

TARTS

16 (3-inch) pie shells

¼ cup white coating chocolate, melted

1½ pounds fresh strawberries (approximately 32), tops and stems removed

½ cup store-bought strawberry glaze

¼ cup croquant, optional (something crispy or crunchy, such as finely chopped nuts, mini chocolate morsels, crumbled shortbread cookies, etc.)

Storytellers Cafe at Disney's Grand Californian Hotel & Spa, 2014

CHAPTER THREE
Across the Disneyland Resort

CHARRED NEBRASKA CORN CHOWDER

Thick and chunky, this meal in a bowl is always on the menu at Storytellers Cafe. Though most chowders are made with seafood, this creamy version is flavored with chicken and bacon.

SERVES 4-6　　　**A DISNEY CLASSIC**

- 4 ears fresh corn, unshucked
- 4 slices bacon, divided
- 1 tablespoon diced onion
- 1 teaspoon chopped garlic
- 1 Yukon Gold potato, peeled and diced
- 4 cups chicken stock
- 6 tablespoons butter
- 6 tablespoons all-purpose flour
- 2 cups heavy cream
- 1 cup pulled chicken meat
- coarse salt, to taste
- freshly ground black pepper, to taste
- hot sauce, to taste
- 2 teaspoons chopped cilantro, for garnish

1. Preheat oven to 350°F. To roast the corn, put whole ears in their husks into preheated oven for 25 minutes. Cool briefly, then peel back the husks and cut the kernels off the cobs; set aside.

2. Dice 2 slices of bacon sauté. Drain all but 1 tablespoon of the fat and add onion and garlic and sauté until transparent but not brown. Add the roasted corn, potato, and chicken stock. Bring to a simmer.

3. Meanwhile melt butter over medium heat in a separate sauté pan. Add flour, mixing with a wire whisk until smooth. Cook 3 to 4 minutes, stirring, until mixture begins to loosen slightly. Let cool.

4. Add the cooled butter/flour mixture to the simmering broth, mixing with a whisk. Stir often to keep from sticking to the bottom of the pan. Simmer 30 to 40 minutes.

5. Add the cream and pulled chicken meat and simmer for another 10 minutes.

6. Meanwhile, cook the remaining bacon until crisp. Drain and chop into small pieces; set aside.

7. Add salt, pepper, and hot sauce to taste. Ladle into bowls and top with garnish of bacon and cilantro.

NAPA ROSE LAVOSH

This easy-to-make bread is a signature part of the bread basket at Napa Rose—and one of the restaurant's most requested recipes.

SERVES A CROWD   **A DISNEY CLASSIC**

1. In bowl, mix olive oil, garlic, and parsley; season with salt and pepper.

2. Brush lavosh with olive oil mixture and sprinkle with cheese.

3. Bake at 350°F for 8 minutes, or until golden brown and lightly crisp. Serve warm, or cooled, as a cracker, with appetizers.

1 cup extra-virgin olive oil

2 large cloves garlic, smashed

2 teaspoons finely chopped parsley

coarse salt, to taste

freshly ground black pepper, to taste

1 package lavosh (This flatbread can be purchased in Indian and other specialty food markets.)

1 cup grated Parmigiano-Reggiano cheese

ROBUSTO FLATBREAD

This flavorful flatbread is a hit at Storytellers Cafe, where the restaurant's expansive wall murals celebrate legendary tales set in California. Burrata, noted in this recipe, is a fresh Italian cheese made from mozzarella and cream. Fresh mozzarella may be substituted.

MAKES 2 (9×12-INCH) FLATBREADS   **SAVORY BITES**

FOR FLATBREAD

1. Preheat oven to 450°F. Season potatoes, toss with oil, and roast for 10 to 15 minutes. Cool potatoes on pan; set aside.

2. Place dough on a floured surface, cut into two equal pieces, and roll and stretch each into a rough circle. Place each dough round on a baking sheet lightly coated with cornmeal. Bake for 3 minutes, or until just beginning to crisp.

3. Remove flatbreads, and top each with a thin layer of romesco sauce. Evenly divide the burrata cheese and blue cheese between flatbreads; sprinkle each evenly with mozzarella. On each flatbread, alternate rows of potatoes and chorizo across the top.

4. Bake flatbreads for 4 to 6 minutes, or until the dough is crisp and cheeses are melted. Sprinkle with fresh thyme and basil. Serve immediately.

FOR ROMESCO SAUCE

1. Combine roasted tomatoes, roasted red peppers, paprika, almonds, and vinegar in a food processor; pulse for 15 seconds.

2. Add olive oil and pulse for 10 seconds. Add bread cubes and pulse until sauce is still slightly chunky but no large pieces of bread remain. Season with salt and pepper to taste.

ROBUSTO FLATBREAD

½ cup fingerling potatoes, sliced into ⅛-inch-thick rounds

coarse salt and freshly ground black pepper, to taste

1 tablespoon olive oil

1 pound prepared pizza dough

Cornmeal for dusting, optional

½ cup romesco sauce, divided

⅔ cup 1-inch cubes burrata cheese

¼ cup crumbled blue cheese

½ cup shredded mozzarella cheese

⅔ cup ⅛-inch-thick sliced chorizo, browned and drained

2 tablespoons fresh thyme

2 tablespoons fresh chopped basil

ROMESCO SAUCE

1 pound tomatoes, seeded, roasted, and peeled

1 pound red bell peppers, roasted, peeled, and seeded

1 tablespoon paprika

¾ cup sliced almonds, toasted

½ cup red wine vinegar

¾ cup olive oil

½ cup French bread cubes, toasted

coarse salt and freshly ground black pepper, to taste

BLACKBERRY MOJITO

Napa Rose at Disney's Grand Californian Hotel & Spa has more certified sommeliers than any other restaurant in the world. Beyond wine, cool cocktails add sparkle to vacation time. Now you can get your own party started with this delicious blend.

SERVES 1

COCKTAIL

3 fresh blackberries

2 lime wedges

4 small mint leaves

½ ounce simple syrup (agave nectar can be substituted)

2 ounces vodka, Stoli Blakberi Vodka preferred

4 ounces soda water

Muddle blackberries, lime, mint, and simple syrup in a cocktail shaker. Add vodka and ice; shake, then top with soda water. Serve in a tall glass.

BELOW: Outdoor patio dining at Napa Rose.

STRAWBERRY BASIL LEMONADE

STARTERS

A fresh and fruity libation for a warm day!

SERVES 1   **COCKTAIL**

Mix all ingredients with ice in a cocktail shaker. Serve in a tall glass.

2 ounces vodka

1 ounce strawberry daiquiri mix or strawberry puree

2 strawberries, hulled and cut into quarters

2 basil leaves, torn in half

4 ounces lemonade

BLACKBERRY ZINFANDEL BRAISED SHORT RIBS

Elegant Napa Rose, named after California's most famous valley of vineyards, serves this hearty dish that's perfect for an informal dinner party. You can make this long-simmered creation a day ahead and then reheat.

SERVES 6　　　　　　**A DISNEY CLASSIC**

12 (6- to 8-ounce) bone-in short ribs

coarse salt, to taste

cracked black pepper, to taste

¼ cup olive oil

1 large onion, diced

2 large carrots, coarsely sliced

1 (4-inch) fennel bulb, sliced

1 bottle red Zinfandel

4 cups veal demi-glace (available at gourmet markets)

2 cups chicken stock

1 (14-ounce) bag frozen blackberries, thawed

4 fresh thyme sprigs

5 fresh sage leaves

½ pint fresh blackberries, for garnish

1. Season short ribs with salt and pepper; refrigerate for 1 hour.

2. Heat olive oil in a large sauté pan over medium-high heat. Brown seasoned short ribs on all sides. Remove from pan and set aside.

3. Add the onion, carrots, and fennel to the sauté pan. Reduce heat to medium and slowly brown vegetables, stirring occasionally.

4. Once all vegetables are evenly browned, add Zinfandel and simmer until the liquid is reduced by 75 percent. Transfer vegetable-wine mixture and short ribs into a stock pot.

5. Add demi-glace, chicken stock, thawed blackberries, thyme, and sage to the short ribs and wine. There should be enough liquid to cover the ribs completely.

6. Bring to a boil; reduce heat to a slow simmer. Continue simmering for 3 hours, or until ribs are tender.

7 Remove ribs from liquid and remove bones from the short ribs. Place ribs in serving pan, cover with foil, and set aside. Continue simmering liquid until reduced to sauce consistency, about 20 minutes.

8 Strain sauce if desired, or simply remove herbs. Ladle over short ribs and garnish with fresh blackberries.

GOOFY'S KITCHEN CHERRY TOMATO AND BOCCONCINI SALAD

MAINS AND SIDES

Goofy's Kitchen is always about family and friends sharing a good laugh over a mix and match of fun foods. This fondly remembered combo of tomatoes and mozzarella cheese makes for the perfect quick and easy salad. Bocconcini are egg-sized mozzarella balls, but you can use any sort of fresh mozzarella in this salad.

SERVES 6   **LEFT THE MENU BUT NOT FORGOTTEN**

- ⅓ cup thinly sliced red onion
- 2 tablespoons golden balsamic vinegar or sherry balsamic vinegar, divided
- 4 cups cherry tomatoes, halved
- 2 cups bocconcini, drained and halved
- 2 tablespoons thinly sliced basil
- 2 tablespoons olive oil
- 1 teaspoon coarse salt
- ¼ teaspoon freshly ground black pepper

1 Combine onions and 1 tablespoon vinegar in a medium bowl; toss to combine. Set aside for 20 minutes. Drain onions from vinegar and set aside; discard vinegar.

2 Combine tomatoes and bocconcini in a large bowl. Add remaining 1 tablespoon vinegar, drained onions, basil, and olive oil. Season with salt and pepper and toss to combine.

CHOCOLATE MARTINI

This liquid dessert is a favorite after-dinner indulgence, with a delectable trio of chocolate, hazelnut, and vanilla. A hint when shaking cocktails: fill the shaker about three-quarters full of ice, leaving room for ingredients to move around inside.

SERVES 1

COCKTAIL

1 ounce chocolate liqueur

½ ounce vanilla vodka

½ ounce hazelnut liqueur

½ ounce clear cacao liqueur

chocolate stick, for garnish

1 Combine ingredients in an ice-filled shaker, shake, and strain into martini glass.

2 Garnish with chocolate stick, if desired.

BANANA SPICED RUM MARTINI

With the rich, smooth flavors of cream, cinnamon, vanilla, banana, and rum, this sweet cocktail pairs well with dessert—or it can stand on its own as a sophisticated final course.

SERVES 1

COCKTAIL

1 ounce horchata cream liqueur

1 ounce spiced rum

1 ounce banana liqueur

Combine ingredients in an ice-filled shaker, shake well, and strain into martini glass.

McINTOSH APPLE CHARLOTTES

This fancy version of an apple pie is made with brioche instead of piecrust, but has the flavor and gooey texture of a traditional pie. At Napa Rose, where the menu is seasonal and celebrates the bounty of California, they serve it with house-made caramel goat cheese ice cream.

SERVES 12

LEFT THE MENU BUT NOT FORGOTTEN

McINTOSH APPLE CHARLOTTES

3 tablespoons unsalted butter

½ cup brown sugar

1 pinch salt

5 large McIntosh apples, peeled, cored, and chopped

½ lemon, juiced and zested

¼ teaspoon vanilla

1 tablespoon apple brandy

12 ½-inch-thick slices brioche

FOR McINTOSH APPLE CHARLOTTES

1. Preheat oven to 350°F. Heat butter, sugar, and salt in a medium skillet over medium heat for 3 to 5 minutes. Add apples, lemon zest, and vanilla; sauté for 5 minutes. Add apple brandy and lemon juice and remove from heat.

2. Grease a 12-well muffin tin with butter.

3. Roll brioche slices with rolling pin until ⅛ inch thick. Place into greased muffin tin to form 12 bowls. Pour apple mixture into centers of brioche bowls.

4. Bake for 8 to 10 minutes, or until the edges are golden brown.

5. Cool for 30 minutes, then carefully remove from muffin tin.

FOR CRUMB TOPPING

1. Preheat oven to 300°F. Combine flour and butter with a pastry blender or 2 knives to form a coarse meal. Add brown sugar, pecans, cinnamon, nutmeg, and vanilla extract; mix until dough forms.

2. Break dough into small pieces on a sheet pan. Bake for 15 to 20 minutes, until golden brown.

3. Sprinkle on top of warm charlottes. Serve with whipped cream or vanilla ice cream.

CRUMB TOPPING

½ cup all-purpose flour

¼ cup unsalted butter, softened

2 tablespoons brown sugar

¼ cup chopped pecans

⅛ teaspoon ground cinnamon

⅛ teaspoon ground nutmeg

½ teaspoon vanilla extract

whipped cream or vanilla ice cream, for serving

SCHARFFEN BERGER CHOCOLATE TRUFFLE CAKE

SWEET ENDINGS AND DESSERTS

Nothing could be more luxurious than this dessert. If you can't find Scharffen Berger chocolate, any high-quality bittersweet (at least 58 percent) chocolate will work. Delicious with vanilla or vanilla-cherry ice cream.

MAKES 8 CAKES　　　　**A DISNEY CLASSIC**

½ cup plus 6 tablespoons unsalted butter, softened (extra for ramekins)

6½ ounces Scharffen Berger bittersweet chocolate, chopped fine

5 large eggs, room temperature, separated

½ cups sugar, divided (extra for ramekins)

1 tablespoon all-purpose flour, sifted

1　Preheat oven to 375°F. Lightly butter bottom and sides of 8 individual 6-ounce ramekins. Coat thinly with sugar and shake out excess. Set aside.

2　Prepare a double boiler and bring water to a simmer over low heat. Place butter and chocolate in top of a double boiler and gently stir until melted smoothly and combined.

3　Whisk egg yolks and ¼ cup sugar in a large mixing bowl for 3 to 4 minutes or until smooth and slightly thickened. Add flour and combine.

4　Ladle a small amount of melted chocolate into egg yolk mixture and whisk to combine. Add another ladle of chocolate into egg yolk mixture and continue to whisk. Once the temperature of the egg yolk mixture has been warmed, add remaining chocolate to egg yolks and whisk vigorously until completely combined. Set aside.

5　Warm egg whites in a small metal bowl (first make sure it is very clean and dry) that just fits into a small saucepan with hot water in it. Allow eggs to warm for 1 to 2 minutes. Remove and add 1 tablespoon sugar, whip mixture using a handheld mixture on medium speed until soft peaks form.

6   Slowly add an additional 1 ½ tablespoons sugar while continuing to whip egg whites. Increase speed to high and slowly add remaining 1 ½ tablespoons sugar. Whip egg whites and sugar for another 3 to 4 minutes or until stiff peaks form.

7   Gently fold in ¼ of chocolate mixture into egg whites to combine. Add remaining chocolate and continue to fold till completely combined, being careful not to overwork mixture.

8   Divide batter equally among the prepared ramekins, filling ¾ full. Place on a baking sheet and bake for 14 minutes, or until tops are puffy, but center is still soft. Do not overbake.

9   Cut around edges of cakes using a small knife to loosen cakes. Carefully invert cakes onto severing plates and serve immediately.

STRAWBERRY CHEESECAKE

Casual California cuisine is on the menu at Storytellers Cafe. This popular item on the dessert buffet took advantage of the Golden State's year-round abundance of strawberries.

MAKES 18 MINI CHEESECAKES   **LEFT THE MENU BUT NOT FORGOTTEN**

FOR CHEESECAKES

1. Preheat oven to 300°F. Combine graham cracker crumbs, brown sugar, and butter in a medium bowl, blending until well combined. Set aside.

2. Beat cream cheese and sugar together until smooth and light. Beat in strawberry jam. Scrape down sides of bowl. Add eggs, one at a time, blending well after each.

3. Divide mixture evenly among three 6-well standard muffin tins. Top each cake with 1 tablespoon of graham cracker crumb mixture.

4. Place muffin tins inside a large roasting pan. Pour hot water into roasting pan to reach halfway up sides of muffin cups. Bake 25 to 30 minutes, or until centers are almost set.

5. Remove from oven and refrigerate at least 2 hours before unmolding and serving.

FOR STRAWBERRY SAUCE

1. Combine strawberries, sugar, and lemon juice in a blender.

2. Puree until smooth; pour sauce through a fine-mesh sieve. Serve with cheesecakes.

STRAWBERRY CHEESECAKES

1 cup graham cracker crumbs

2 tablespoons brown sugar

3 tablespoons unsalted butter, melted

3 (8-ounce) packages cream cheese, softened

½ cup sugar

2 tablespoons strawberry jam

3 eggs

STRAWBERRY SAUCE

1 pint fresh strawberries, cored and quartered

3 teaspoons sugar

1 tablespoon fresh lemon juice

Cinderella Castle, 2021

CHAPTER FOUR
Magic Kingdom

SEASONAL VEGETABLE POTPIE WITH HERBED BISCUIT TOPPING

This savory potpie was a popular meal in the charming Liberty Tree Tavern. This vegan dish is topped with a signature flour biscuit flavored with fresh basil, thyme, and rosemary.

SERVES 6–8   **LEFT THE MENU BUT NOT FORGOTTEN**

FOR VEGETABLE FILLING

1 Preheat oven to 350°F. Combine 3 tablespoons olive oil and flour in a medium saucepan. Cook over medium-high heat, whisking constantly, until mixture begins to bubble and starts to thicken, and coat the bottom of the pan, about 5 minutes. Be careful not to let the flour burn.

2 When flour mixture begins to thicken, stir in vegetable stock and whisk until mixture is smooth. Bring to a boil and then reduce to a simmer. Cook, stirring occasionally, until mixture is thickened to a gravy-like consistency, about 10 to 12 minutes.

3 Add dill, sage, and thyme leaves. Stir well to combine and season to taste. Remove from heat and set aside.

4 Heat remaining 1 tablespoon of olive oil over medium-high heat in a large skillet. Add onion, garlic, celery, and carrot and cook until onion is beginning to soften and is translucent, about 3 to 5 minutes.

5 Add zucchini, yellow squash, and green beans. Cook, stirring frequently, until beginning to soften, about 3 to 5 minutes.

VEGETABLE FILLING

4 tablespoons extra-virgin olive oil, divided

3 tablespoons all-purpose flour

2 cups vegetable stock

1½ teaspoons finely chopped fresh dill

1½ teaspoons finely chopped fresh sage leaves

1 teaspoon fresh thyme leaves

1 medium onion, finely chopped

2 cloves garlic, finely chopped

2 stalks celery, thickly sliced

2 peeled carrots, thickly sliced

1 zucchini, quartered lengthwise and cut into ½-inch pieces

1 yellow squash, quartered lengthwise and cut into ½-inch pieces

1 cup green beans, trimmed to ½-inch pieces

1 cup peas (can be frozen)

2 cups cooked navy beans (can be canned)

coarse salt and freshly ground black pepper, to taste

6   Add peas, navy beans, and reserved thickened vegetable broth. Stir all together until well combined. Remove from heat.

7   Let cool slightly and transfer to a 9 × 13-inch baking dish. Set aside.

(RECIPE CONTINUES ON PAGE 58)

SEASONAL VEGETABLE POTPIE WITH HERBED BISCUIT TOPPING

(CONTINUED)

FOR BISCUIT TOPPING

1 Stir together flour, salt, baking powder, pepper, basil, thyme, and rosemary in a large mixing bowl until well combined.

2 Stir in milk and oils. Stir until mixture is just combined, being careful not to overmix.

3 Drop in large spoonfuls on top of vegetable mixture.

4 Cook for 45 minutes to 1 hour, until biscuits are golden brown.

5 Serve warm with a dollop of tomato pistou on top of each serving.

FOR TOMATO PISTOU

1 Combine tomatoes, garlic, basil, sugar, salt, and pepper in a food processor or blender fitted with a metal blade. Pulse until coarsely chopped.

2 Add vinegar and oil, and pulse until mixture is fully combined. The pistou will not be smooth; the consistency will be coarse.

3 Serve as an accompaniment to the potpie.

BISCUIT TOPPING

3 cups all-purpose flour

1 ½ teaspoons coarse salt

1 tablespoon baking powder

½ teaspoon freshly ground black pepper

2 tablespoons finely chopped fresh basil

2 tablespoons fresh thyme leaves

2 tablespoons finely chopped fresh rosemary

¾ cup rice milk

¼ cup canola oil

½ cup extra-virgin olive oil

TOMATO PISTOU

¼ cup sun-dried tomatoes in oil

1 clove garlic, peeled

1 tablespoon finely chopped fresh basil leaves

1 teaspoon sugar

¼ teaspoon coarse salt

¼ teaspoon freshly ground black pepper

2 teaspoons balsamic vinegar

¼ cup extra-virgin olive oil

EDAMAME SALAD

The Crystal Palace, an ornate glass-ceilinged landmark in the Magic Kingdom, is a favorite spot to meet and greet Disney characters. Its food offerings change seasonally, often with creative salads on the menu.

For this dish, edamame can be found in most supermarkets in the frozen-fresh sections. Daikon radishes are often in the supermarket, or you can find them at the local Asian grocery. (Red radishes are not a good substitute.)

SERVES 4-6　　　　**LEFT THE MENU BUT NOT FORGOTTEN**

4 cups edamame (young soybeans), fresh or frozen

½ cup rice wine vinegar

¼ cup sesame oil

1 teaspoon coarse salt

1 cup chopped napa cabbage

½ cup chopped bok choy

½ cup shredded carrots

1 tablespoon black sesame seeds

¼ cup shredded white daikon radish

1　Cook fresh or frozen beans in boiling salted water for 3 minutes, then chill.

2　In a small mixing bowl, combine vinegar, sesame oil, salt, napa cabbage, and bok choy. Let sit at room temperature for 20 minutes. (Cabbage will wilt slightly.)

3　Mix in carrots, then refrigerate for 1 hour.

4　To serve, top with sesame seeds and daikon radish.

© Disney

GREY STUFF

"Try the grey stuff," sings Lumiere. First served up in the film *Beauty and the Beast* (1991), the "stuff" is now a treat in the Magic Kingdom. Part of the fun is not knowing exactly what is in the creamy concoction.

Until now. Distinguished guests, we present . . . your dessert . . . at Be Our Guest Restaurant!

MAKES 12　　　　　　**A DISNEY CLASSIC**

1½ cups cold whole milk

1 (3.4-ounce) package instant vanilla pudding mix

15 chocolate sandwich cookies

1 (8-ounce) container whipped topping, thawed

3 tablespoons instant chocolate pudding mix

12 scalloped sugar cookies

edible sugar pearls

1　Pour milk into large mixing bowl. Add vanilla pudding mix and whisk for 2 minutes, until smooth and slightly thickened. Refrigerate 1 to 2 hours or until firm.

2　Pulse chocolate sandwich cookies in food processor until pureed. Fold into pudding mix, stirring until fully mixed.

3　Stir in whipped topping and chocolate pudding mix, mixing well. Refrigerate for 1 hour.

4　Spoon into piping bag fitted with desired tip and pipe onto sugar cookies. Top with sugar pearls.

OPPOSITE, BOTTOM: Exterior detail atop the cliff-side entrance to Be Our Guest Restaurant.

LEMON CURD CREAM PUFFS

Step inside the Beast's enchanted castle, where dishes such as these cream puffs are inspired by French cuisine. You can make a gluten-free version of the puffs with gluten-free flour, one additional egg, and no sugar dough. Or for a slightly less sweet puff, just omit the sugar dough and lightly smooth the tops of the puffs with a damp fingertip before baking.

MAKES APPROXIMATELY 28 PUFFS   **A DISNEY CLASSIC**

SUGAR DOUGH

½ cup (1 stick) unsalted butter, at room temperature

½ cup sugar

½ cup all-purpose flour

CREAM PUFFS

1 cup plus 2 tablespoons water

½ cup (1 stick) unsalted butter

1½ teaspoons sugar

1 pinch salt

1 cup all-purpose flour, sifted

6 eggs

FOR SUGAR DOUGH

1   Combine butter, sugar, and flour in a bowl and mix until dough comes together. Place on one half of a large piece of plastic wrap. Fold wrap over dough and gently press into a ¼-inch-thick round.

2   Refrigerate and chill at least 1 hour.

FOR CREAM PUFFS

1   Preheat oven to 350°F. Line 2 large baking sheets with parchment paper and set aside.

2   Combine water, butter, sugar, and salt in a medium saucepan over high heat and bring to a boil.

3   Remove from heat. Using a wooden spoon, quickly stir in flour.

4   Place saucepan over medium-high heat and continue stirring vigorously until mixture pulls away from sides and forms a ball, about 2 minutes.

5 Transfer to bowl of an electric mixer fitted with a paddle attachment and mix on low speed until slightly cooled, about 2 minutes.

6 Raise speed to medium; add eggs, one at a time, beating until dough comes back together before adding next egg. Beat until a soft peak forms, about 2 minutes.

7 Transfer batter into a large zip-top bag, squeezing dough into bottom corner of bag. Snip tip off corner and use bag to pipe 2-inch dots of batter onto prepared baking sheets.

8 Working quickly, roll sugar dough in plastic wrap to ⅛-inch thickness.

9 Cut into 2-inch circles and use a butter knife to transfer circles to tops of puffs.

10 Bake for 35 to 40 minutes, or until tops are golden brown. Set aside to cool before filling.

FOR LEMON CURD:

1 Fill a medium saucepan with a few inches of water and place over medium-high heat.

2 Combine egg yolks and sugar in a heatproof bowl that's slightly bigger than the saucepan; place bowl over saucepan. Whisk 1 minute, then add lemon juice. Whisk 6 to 8 minutes, until mixture thickens.

3 Remove from heat, and add butter 1 piece at a time, stirring until fully melted before adding next piece.

4 Transfer to a clean bowl and cover by placing a piece of plastic wrap directly onto the surface. Refrigerate until cold.

5 Use the tip of a paring knife to make a small X in the bottom of each puff. Fill the corner of a large resealable zip-top bag with lemon curd. Snip the tip off the corner of the bag and pipe curd into each puff.

LEMON CURD

6 egg yolks

1 cup sugar

⅓ cup fresh lemon juice (from about 4 lemons)

½ cup (1 stick) unsalted butter, cubed

Spaceship Earth, 2020

CHAPTER FIVE

EPCOT

CHARRED SKIRT STEAK, CORN PANCAKES, JICAMA SLAW

This dish debuted at the Flavors from Fire Marketplace at the EPCOT International Food & Wine Festival. If you don't have time to make the corn pancakes, you can serve with store-bought corn tortillas. Carefully fry them in a heavy skillet over medium-high heat with 2 tablespoons hot oil for about 10 to 30 seconds on each side until browned and cooked. (They will still be pliable.) Drain on paper towels and keep warm until ready to serve.

SERVES 6 **FESTIVAL FAVORITE TO REMEMBER**

FOR MARINATED SKIRT STEAK

1 Place all ingredients except steak in blender and puree until smooth.

2 Taste and adjust seasonings.

3 Put steak in large zip-top bag and add marinade. Refrigerate several hours or overnight.

FOR JICAMA SLAW

1 Julienne jicama and carrots with mandoline and place in glass bowl. Add onion and diced pepper.

2 Blend vinegar, salt, pepper, and sugar at medium speed in blender.

3 With blender running, slowly add oil.

MARINATED SKIRT STEAK

3 tablespoons chopped flat-leaf parsley

3 tablespoons chopped cilantro

¼ teaspoon dried oregano

1 teaspoon minced garlic

½ teaspoon chopped Fresno or jalapeño pepper

¼ teaspoon chopped serrano pepper

2 tablespoons diced red onion

1 pinch coarse salt

1 pinch freshly ground black pepper

1 pinch smoked Spanish paprika

1 pinch chili flakes

2 tablespoons red wine vinegar

¼ cup canola oil

1 pound skirt steak

JICAMA SLAW

1 cup peeled jicama, julienned with mandoline

½ cup peeled carrots, julienned with mandoline

¼ cup red onion, thinly sliced, about 2-inch-long pieces

1 teaspoon finely diced Fresno or jalapeño pepper

4 Stir in parsley and adjust seasonings. Pour dressing over slaw.

5 Transfer to glass bowl or zip-top bag and marinate in refrigerator at least 4 hours.

FOR CILANTRO CREAM

1 Combine all ingredients in blender and puree until smooth. Adjust seasoning if necessary.

2 Transfer to bowl, cover, and refrigerate for at least 1 hour.

FOR CORN PANCAKES

1 Smoke corn over hickory wood chips at 220°F for 20 minutes. Remove from heat, cool, and cut kernels from cob. Divide into 2 equal portions.

2 Puree egg, water, milk, salt, pepper, and half of corn in food processor until smooth.

3 Transfer to medium-size bowl and fold in masa harina and remaining corn.

4 Heat canola oil in a medium-size skillet over medium-high heat. Pour a heaping tablespoon of batter into skillet and spread about ¼-inch thickness. Cook for about 4 minutes or until golden brown, flipping halfway through. Cook in batches and keep warm until ready to serve. (This step can be done while steak is resting.)

TO SERVE

1 Remove steak from marinade and grill over charcoal to medium rare. Remove from heat and rest 10 minutes. Slice thinly against grain.

2 Place pancake on serving plate, and top with steaks, slaw, and cilantro cream.

1 cup white vinegar

1 teaspoon coarse salt

1 pinch freshly ground black pepper

3 tablespoons sugar

2 teaspoons canola oil

¼ teaspoon chopped flat-leaf parsley

CILANTRO CREAM

¼ cup sour cream

½ cup mayonnaise

1 to 2 tablespoons chopped cilantro

2 tablespoons lime juice

1 teaspoon minced garlic

1 pinch coarse salt

CORN PANCAKES

2 large ears yellow corn, shucked

1 large egg

3 tablespoons water

3 tablespoons whole milk

1 pinch coarse salt

1 pinch freshly ground black pepper

½ cup masa harina

1 teaspoon canola oil, more as needed

LAMB MEATBALL WITH SPICY TOMATO CHUTNEY

New Zealand has been part of the EPCOT International Food & Wine Festival since 1997, and as New Zealanders love their lamb, it's been featured on every Marketplace menu. These tender meatballs, topped with a sweet and savory tomato chutney, were a guest favorite in 2012. Add more chili flakes to the chutney if you prefer a little more heat. The meatballs are served in a small popover for easy eating at the festival.

SERVES 4   **FESTIVAL FAVORITE TO REMEMBER**

FOR LAMB MEATBALLS

1 Preheat oven to 350°F. Carefully heat oil in large sauté pan over medium heat. Add onions and garlic, cooking until translucent. Add thyme, rosemary, chili flakes, and cumin; cook 2 minutes more.

2 Add tomatoes, cooking until mixture is combined and vegetables are soft. Season with salt and pepper. Transfer to a large bowl and set aside until cooled to room temperature.

3 Place bread in a small bowl; add enough cool water to cover. Soak 10 minutes.

4 Squeeze water out of bread, Place soaked bread in bowl with onion mixture. Add ground lamb and mix to combine. Form into 12 meatballs.

LAMB MEATBALLS

2 tablespoons extra-virgin olive oil

½ cup finely chopped onion

2 cloves garlic, chopped

½ teaspoon chopped fresh thyme

½ teaspoon chopped fresh rosemary

¼ teaspoon chili flakes

¼ teaspoon ground cumin

½ cup finely chopped fresh tomatoes

coarse salt, to taste

freshly ground black pepper, to taste

1 cup torn French bread, without crust

½ pound ground lamb

OPPOSITE, RIGHT: Park entrance during the EPCOT International Food & Wine Festival, 2018

5 Bake 20 minutes; remove from oven and keep warm until ready to serve.

FOR SPICY TOMATO CHUTNEY

1 Combine all ingredients except salt in a small saucepan over high heat and bring to boil.

2 Reduce heat to medium-low and simmer 45 to 60 minutes, or until chutney is thick, Season with salt.

TO SERVE

Place 3 meatballs on a small plate; top with a spoonful of chutney. Serve warm.

SPICY TOMATO CHUTNEY

½ cup chopped onion

6 plum tomatoes, chopped

¼ cup white wine vinegar

2 tablespoons light brown sugar

1 teaspoon sugar

1 tablespoon minced garlic

5 leaves fresh basil

2 sprigs fresh thyme

½ teaspoon chili flakes

coarse salt, to taste

GRASS-FED BEEF SLIDERS WITH PIMENTO CHEESE

STARTERS

All-American tastes like barbecue, crab cakes, and lobster rolls have been on tap at Hops & Barley Marketplace since its debut in 2005. The grass-fed beef burger, which was included on the Marketplace menu in 2014 and 2015, is the perfect accompaniment to an ice-cold beer. Forget a slice of melted cheese on top; slather with this spicy pimento cheese instead.

MAKES 12 SLIDERS

FESTIVAL FAVORITE TO REMEMBER

FOR PIMENTO CHEESE

1. Place all ingredients in a food processor and mix thoroughly. Do not over-process. (Mixture should be lumpy.)

2. Refrigerate for at least 1 hour.

FOR SLIDERS

1. Preheat grill to medium-high heat.

2. Butter both sides of bun and toast on grill. Set aside.

3. Cook sliders to desired doneness. Place sliders on bottom halves of buns.

4. Top with a liberal amount of pimento cheese and top with remaining halves of buns. Serve immediately.

PIMENTO CHEESE

2 cups extra-sharp cheddar cheese, shredded

8 ounces cream cheese

½ cup mayonnaise

½ cup roasted red peppers, finely diced

¼ teaspoon ground cayenne pepper

1 cup favorite spice relish, drained

1 jalapeño pepper, finely diced

coarse salt, to taste

freshly ground black pepper, to taste

SLIDERS

1½ pounds grass-fed beef, formed into 12 (2-ounce) patties

12 slider buns

½ cup butter, melted

POTATO PANCAKES WITH CHIVE SOUR CREAM

This savory appetizer is paired at EPCOT International Food & Wine Festival with a sparkling brut wine. The starchier the potato, the crisper the potato pancake: use the classic Idaho or russet.

SERVES 4-6

FESTIVAL FAVORITE TO REMEMBER

CHIVE SOUR CREAM

½ cup sour cream

1 bundle chives, finely chopped (at least 2 tablespoons)

coarse salt, to taste

freshly ground black pepper, to taste

juice from 1 lemon, optional

POTATO PANCAKES

1 pound classic Idaho or russet potatoes, peeled

1 small onion

2 eggs

3 tablespoons flour

coarse salt, to taste

vegetable oil for frying

FOR CHIVE SOUR CREAM

Mix ingredients together in a small bowl.

FOR POTATO PANCAKES

1 Coarsely grate potatoes and onion with box grater or food processor fitted with grating disk. Press potatoes and onions to extract as much liquid as possible.

2 Stir potatoes and onions with eggs and flour in a large bowl. (Mix well, but don't overwork.) Season with salt.

3 Heat 3 tablespoons oil in large, heavy skillet. When hot enough to sizzle a drop of water, carefully drop a tablespoonful of potato mixture into skillet, pressing with a spatula to slightly flatten. Cook until golden brown on bottom, about 4 to 5 minutes. Gently flip and cook until golden brown on the other side, 4 to 5 minutes. Repeat with remaining potato mixture and more oil.

4 Transfer to paper towels to drain; season with salt. Keep warm on baking sheets in oven while making remaining pancakes.

5 Serve pancakes hot, drizzled with chive sour cream.

OPPOSITE, BOTTOM: Guests at the EPCOT International Food & Wine Festival, 2021

CITRUS THISTLE

Scotland joined the EPCOT International Food & Wine Festival lineup in 2000 for one year, then returned in 2013. This fresh cocktail debuted in 2015.

SERVES 1   **FESTIVAL FAVORITE TO REMEMBER**

3 ounces Premium Grapefruit Sour Mix

1 ounce gin

fresh basil leaf, for garnish

grapefruit twist, for garnish

1   Fill a shaker glass with ice. Add ingredients and shake well.

2   Pour into a martini glass and garnish with basil and lemon twist.

TZATZIKI MARTINI

The Greece Marketplace, one of the most popular with guests, has been part of the EPCOT International Food & Wine Festival every year except 2001. This cocktail is infused with classic Greek flavors of yogurt, lemon, and dill.

SERVES 1 **FESTIVAL FAVORITE TO REMEMBER**

1 ½ ounces Crop Organic Cucumber Vodka

¾ ounce BOLS Natural Yoghurt Liqueur

½ ounce lemonade

sprig of dill, for garnish

lemon wedge, for garnish

1 Place ice in a chilled cocktail shaker. Add vodka, liqueur, and lemonade; shake for 30 seconds.

2 Strain into a serving glass, garnish with dill and lemon, and serve immediately.

FROZEN DRAGON BERRY COLADA

The Caribbean Marketplace debuted at EPCOT International Food & Wine Festival in 1996 and was changed to Floribbean from 1997 to 1999. After a hiatus, the Caribbean Marketplace was back from 2011 to 2012 with this sweet cocktail paired with island flavors.

2 ounces Bacardi Dragon Berry Rum

2 ounces strawberry puree

3 ounces piña colada mix

Wedges of pineapple and dragon fruit, for garnish

SERVES 1   **FESTIVAL FAVORITE TO REMEMBER**

1 Pour Bacardi Dragon Berry, strawberry puree, and piña colada mix into blender with 1 cup of ice; blend until smooth.

2 Pour into tall glass and garnish with wedges of pineapple and dragon fruit.

GLÜHWEIN (HOT SPICE WINE)

In wintertime, whimsical overlays transform iconic architecture during the EPCOT International Festival of the Holidays. Each of the eleven World Showcase countries offers a taste of home to guests with cultural sights, sounds, and flavors. This hot spice wine harkens from the Bavaria Holiday Kitchen at the Germany pavilion.

SERVES 1   **FESTIVAL FAVORITE TO REMEMBER**

1 bottle (750 ml) Cabernet Sauvignon

½ cup sugar

3 whole cloves

2 sticks cinnamon

2 star anise pods

1 orange, cut into slices

1. Combine all ingredients in a pot over medium heat. Bring to a gentle simmer, reduce heat, and simmer for 30 minutes.

2. Turn off heat and let wine continue to steep for 30 minutes. (Taste and adjust sugar.) Put a strainer over mugs to remove spices, and serve warm.

PORK GOULASH PIEROGI

MAINS AND SIDES

Part of the EPCOT International Food & Wine Festival Marketplace lineup since 1996, Poland is one of just a handful of countries that can boast that it still serves a dish that has been on the menu since that very first festival: pierogi. This is a rendition of the classic Polish dumpling that debuted at the festival in 2014, stuffed with sauerkraut and served with a rich pork goulash.

SERVES 6-8   **FESTIVAL FAVORITE TO REMEMBER**

FOR PORK GOULASH

1   Heat canola oil in large braising pan over medium-high heat. Add onions and caramelize until lightly browned, about 10 to 12 minutes.

2   Season diced pork with salt, pepper, and 1 tablespoon paprika. Reduce heat to medium and add garlic and seasoned pork to onions. Sauté for 2 minutes.

3   Add bay leaves, caraway seeds, pepper flakes, and remaining paprika. Sauté until meat begins to brown.

4   Add tomato paste and stir until all ingredients are well coated. Dust mixture with flour and stir. Add chicken stock and stir. Reduce heat to simmer and cook for about 30 minutes, stirring occasionally to prevent burning.

5   Add sauerkraut and continue to simmer for about 1½ hours or until meat is tender, stirring occasionally and adding water or chicken stock if mixture needs to be thinned. Goulash should be thick but more sauce-like in consistency. Remove bay leaves.

6   Remove from heat. Cover and set aside until serving.

PORK GOULASH

¼ cup canola oil

1 large Spanish onion, diced

2 pounds pork butt, diced, exterior pieces of fat trimmed

1 teaspoon coarse salt

1 teaspoon freshly ground black pepper

2 tablespoons Hungarian paprika, divided

4 cloves garlic, minced

2 bay leaves

1 teaspoon caraway seeds

½ teaspoon red pepper flakes

1 cup tomato paste

¼ cup flour

1½ cups chicken stock

2 cups sauerkraut, thoroughly drained

FOR SAUERKRAUT PIEROGI

1 Combine flour and salt in large bowl of standing mixer. Blend on low speed using bread hook attachment.

2 Add chicken stock, eggs, and butter. Mix on medium speed until dough forms into ball. Add a bit of water or flour as needed. (Dough can also be made in large food processor.) Cover with plastic wrap and set aside for about 30 minutes.

3 Divide dough into 4 equal parts. On lightly floured surface, roll one portion of dough to ⅛-inch thickness and cut into individual pierogi with floured 3-inch to 4-inch biscuit cutter or mold.

4 Place 1 full tablespoon of drained sauerkraut in center of pierogi. Do not overfill. Moisten edge of half with water and fold over, pressing edges together to form seal. Repeat step with remaining dough and sauerkraut, keeping pierogi covered with damp towel while assembling others.

5 In large pot, bring 2 quarts salted water to boil. Reduce to simmer. Working in batches, cook pierogi for 2 to 3 minutes, or until they surface. Remove from water with slotted spoon and place on tray or plate to dry.

6 Melt butter in large sauté pan or skillet over medium-high heat until butter just begins to brown. Reduce heat to medium and add pierogi to pan. (Number depends on size of pan/skillet.) Cook until lightly browned. Remove from pan and keep warm until all are cooked, adding more butter if needed.

TO SERVE

1 Reheat pork goulash to sauce consistency, adding liquid (water, chicken stock, or red wine) to thin if necessary.

2 Place 3 or 4 cooked pierogi on serving plate and top with goulash. Serve immediately.

SAUERKRAUT PIEROGI

5 cups all-purpose flour

1 teaspoon salt

1 cup water or chicken stock

3 large eggs

½ cup butter, softened

3 cups sauerkraut, thoroughly drained

2 tablespoons butter

NEW ENGLAND LOBSTER ROLL

MAINS AND SIDES

Showcasing American flavors from crab cakes to ribs to bison chili, the American Adventure Marketplace debuted at the EPCOT International Food & Wine Festival in 1996. Renamed the United States Marketplace in 1997, it was part of the festival lineup through 2008, returning once in 2010. This lobster roll was on the menu in 2006.

MAKES 4 LOBSTER ROLLS　　**FESTIVAL FAVORITE TO REMEMBER**

1 Combine lobster meat, onion, red pepper, and celery in a large bowl.

2 Add mayonnaise, mustard, and tarragon; mix thoroughly. Season to taste with salt and pepper.

3 Preheat broiler.

4 Split open each bun and brush inside with 1 tablespoon butter.

5 Place buns on a baking pan, buttered side up, and broil until golden brown.

6 Sprinkle ¼ cup of the lettuce on each bun and top with ½ cup lobster salad.

2 pounds cooked lobster meat, cut into ½-inch chunks

½ cup finely chopped white onion

½ cup finely chopped red bell pepper

½ cup finely chopped celery

¾ cup mayonnaise

1 tablespoon Dijon-style mustard

1 tablespoon finely chopped fresh tarragon

coarse salt, to taste

freshly ground black pepper, to taste

4 hot dog–style buns

4 tablespoons butter, melted

1 cup shredded romaine lettuce

COQUITO

Featured at the Feast of the Three Kings Holiday Kitchen near World Showcase Plaza, coquito is a traditional coconut eggnog punch served at Christmas and New Year's celebrations in Puerto Rico. It's rich and meant to be sipped—and you can always add more rum and sip it on the rocks.

SERVES 6   **FESTIVAL FAVORITE TO REMEMBER**

12 ounces evaporated milk

14 ounces sweetened condensed milk

16 ounces cream of coconut

½ teaspoon ground cinnamon

¼ teaspoon ground nutmeg

6 ounces dark rum

cinnamon sticks, for garnish

additional ground cinnamon, to taste, for garnish

1 Mix evaporated milk, unsweetened condensed milk, cream of coconut, cinnamon, and nutmeg in a blender. Refrigerate for at least 1 hour.

2 Just before serving, add dark rum and give a quick blend.

3 Serve in 8-ounce glasses and garnish each with a cinnamon stick and a pinch of ground cinnamon.

FLORENTINE COOKIES

Yodelers and traditional Bavarian musicians entertain in an Oktoberfest celebration at the Biergarten Restaurant in the Germany pavilion. The recipe for these kid-friendly treats is great for beginning home chefs. If you don't like raspberry jam, you can use your (or your young chef's) favorite flavor.

MAKES 32 (2×3-INCH) COOKIES

LEFT THE MENU BUT NOT FORGOTTEN

1 (16.5-ounce) package refrigerated sugar cookie dough

1 cup raspberry jam

½ cup sliced almonds

½ tablespoon granulated sugar

1 Preheat oven to 350°F. Cut a sheet of parchment paper to fit inside a regular sheet pan. Place the parchment paper rectangle on the counter, and place cookie dough on the parchment paper.

2 Roll out cookie dough to cover most of the rectangle, leaving a ½-inch border of paper. The dough should be approximately ⅛ inch thick.

3 Carefully transfer dough on parchment paper to the sheet pan. Spoon jam onto dough, and use the back of a spoon to spread it evenly over dough. Evenly sprinkle with almonds and sugar.

4 Bake for 15 to 18 minutes. Transfer sheet pan to wire rack to cool completely, at least 1 hour. When cool, slide baked dough off sheet pan. Cut into rectangles using a pizza cutter or a knife.

5 Store cookies in an airtight container, separating layers with pieces of parchment paper to prevent them from sticking together.

POP ART COOKIE

A multifaceted celebration of art in many forms, EPCOT International Festival of the Arts features world-class cuisine, remarkable visual art, and an extraordinary lineup of performance art, music, and hands-on workshops and seminars. Kids have a blast decorating with the glaze on the whimsical cookie. Decorate on parchment or waxed paper. If a fork is too messy for drizzling, use a small zip-top bag and snip off a corner.

MAKES 6 COOKIES   **FESTIVAL FAVORITE TO REMEMBER**

SUGAR COOKIE

½ cup sugar

1 cup butter

1 egg white

2½ cups all-purpose flour, sifted

⅛ teaspoon salt

FOR SUGAR COOKIE

1. Cream sugar and butter until fluffy in bowl of electric mixer fitted with paddle attachment. Add egg white and beat for 1 minute.

2. Slowly add flour and salt and beat at medium speed until soft dough forms.

3. Cover and refrigerate for 30 minutes.

4. Preheat oven to 300°F. Line a baking sheet with parchment or silicone baking mat.

5. Roll dough into a ¼-inch-thick rectangle on a lightly floured surface.

6. Cut into 6 (3×5-inch) rectangles.

7. Place cookies on prepared baking sheet and bake for 15 minutes, or until golden brown.

8. Remove from oven and cool.

FOR TOPPING

Spread 1 tablespoon strawberry jam on each cookie, leaving a border of about ⅛ inch around edges. Set aside.

FOR GLAZE

1. Whisk powdered sugar, 3 tablespoons of milk, and vanilla extract in a pie plate until smooth. (Add additional milk if glaze is too thick.)

2. Set aside 2 tablespoons of glaze in small bowl.

3. Dip each cookie, jam side down, in glaze to cover the jam. Set on a wire rack to dry.

4. Mix remaining glaze with desired colors of food coloring. Use a fork to drizzle on cookies.

TOPPINGS

6 tablespoons strawberry jam

GLAZE

1½ cups powdered sugar

3 to 4 tablespoons milk

2 teaspoons vanilla extract

food coloring

IRISH WHISKEY CUSTARD

Just five ingredients create a decadent, creamy treat with a flourish of Irish whiskey. It was a popular way to end a meal in the Rose & Crown Pub & Dining Room at the United Kingdom pavilion. The décor inside combines styles of several types of classic U.K. pubs— finding inspiration from typical street-side ones in the larger cities and country towns to the likes of the famous Ye Olde Cheshire Cheese in London.

3⅓ cups heavy cream

½ cup half-and-half

⅞ cup plus 8 tablespoons sugar

8 egg yolks

3 tablespoons Irish whiskey

SERVES 8   **LEFT THE MENU BUT NOT FORGOTTEN**

1 Preheat oven to 300°F. Combine all ingredients in a large bowl, except for 8 tablespoons of sugar. Whisk until combined.

2 Pour mixture through a fine mesh strainer into another large bowl. Divide mixture evenly among 8 (8-ounce) custard bowls or ramekins.

3 Place 4 custard bowls into each of 2 (9×13×2-inch) baking pans. Pour water into both pans until level reaches three quarters of the way up sides of custard bowls.

4 Bake for 45 to 50 minutes or until custard is set but not browned.

5 Remove custard bowls from water baths and cool in refrigerator at least 3 hours.

6 To serve, evenly sprinkle top of each custard with 1 tablespoon of remaining sugar. Use a kitchen torch to caramelize the sugar, keeping the flame about 2 inches above surface so sugar melts and browns. Allow sugar to cool and harden for 1 minute before serving.

Slinky Dog Dash at Toy Story Land, 2018

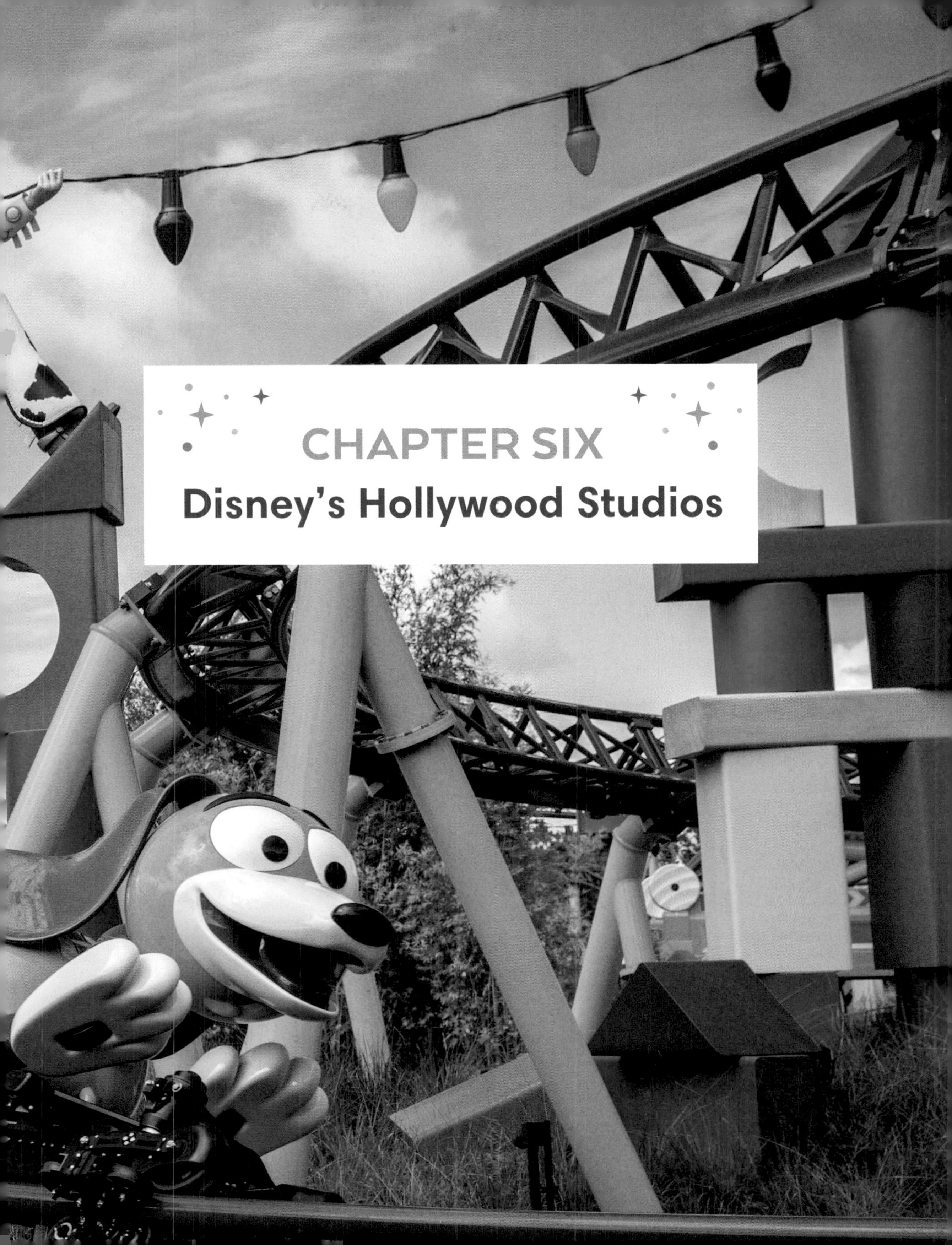

CHAPTER SIX

Disney's Hollywood Studios

TOTCHOS

Woody's Lunch Box, a quick-service restaurant in Toy Story Land, opened in 2018 and is themed to—well, hey howdy hey—a vintage-looking tin lunch box with designs from the mid-twentieth-century show-in-a-show *Woody's Roundup*, which was first introduced to fans in *Toy Story 2* (1999).

SERVES 6

SAVORY BITES

FOR CHILI WITH BEANS

 1 Brown ground beef in a 5- to 6-quart Dutch oven over medium heat until fully cooked. Drain off excess grease.

2 Add onion and garlic and sauté for 5–7 minutes, until onion is translucent.

3 Add crushed tomatoes, tomato sauce, kidney beans, chili powder, and cumin. Simmer for 20 minutes. Add salt.

4 Add black pepper and cayenne as needed.

5 Keep warm until ready to serve.

FOR QUESO SAUCE

 1 Place cheese sauce and diced tomatoes with chilies in small saucepan. Cook over low heat for 10 minutes, until warm.

2 Keep warm until ready to serve.

CHILI WITH BEANS

1 pound lean ground beef

1 medium yellow onion, finely chopped

3 cloves garlic, minced

1 (14.5-ounce) can crushed tomatoes

1 (15-ounce) can tomato sauce

1 (15-ounce) can kidney beans, drained

2 tablespoons chili powder

1 tablespoon ground cumin

1 tablespoon coarse salt

black pepper, to taste

ground cayenne, to taste

QUESO SAUCE

2 cups jar cheese sauce

1 (10-ounce) can diced tomatoes with chilies

FOR TOTCHOS

1 Cook potato barrels according to package instructions.

2 Divide potato barrels into 6 bowls. Place ¼ cup each of corn chips, chili with beans, and queso sauce on top of each bowl of potato barrels.

3 Top each bowl with 2 tablespoons shredded cheese, 1 tablespoon sour cream, and 1 teaspoon green onions.

TOTCHOS

1 (2-pound) bag frozen potato barrels

1 ½ cups corn chips

chili with beans

queso sauce

¾ cup shredded cheddar cheese

6 tablespoons sour cream

2 tablespoons thinly sliced green onions

DAGOBAH SLUG SLINGER

In the lore of *Star Wars*: Galaxy's Edge, a crafty Blutopian named Oga Garra is the proprietor of an influential bar, known as Oga's Cantina, at Black Spire Outpost. While Oga herself mostly runs operations from afar, visiting guests can see up front the Walt Disney Imagineering magic that creates this immersive environment. The name Dagobah in this green beverage, of course, pays homage to the swamp-covered planet Yoda once called home.

SERVES 1

COCKTAIL

½ ounce lime juice

2 ounces orange juice

1 ounce Dagobah Slug Syrup

½ teaspoon blue curaçao

2 ounces tequila

1 ounce water

a sprig of rosemary, for garnish

DAGOBAH SLUG SYRUP

1 cup sugar

1 cup water

4 ounces fresh ginger, peeled and sliced ¼ inch thick

1 (3-inch) rosemary sprig

1 Combine the lime juice, orange juice, Dagobah Slug Syrup, curaçao, tequila, and water in a shaker and give it a few good shakes to combine.

2 Pour into a tall glass with a few ice cubes and garnish with a sprig of rosemary.

3 For added flair, light part of the rosemary sprig on fire, then blow out and let smolder.

FOR DAGOBAH SLUG SYRUP

In a small saucepan over medium heat, bring the sugar and water to a boil. Add the ginger and rosemary and return to a boil, stirring to dissolve the sugar. Remove from the heat and let rest to infuse for at least 5 hours, until very strong. Strain into a clean bottle and refrigerate until ready to use. Keeps for 1 to 2 weeks.

THE HOLLYWOOD BROWN DERBY COBB SALAD

Disney's spin on the classic Cobb salad is the most requested entrée at The Hollywood Brown Derby. The story goes that in 1937, Bob Cobb, owner of the original Brown Derby, and theater magnate Sid Grauman prowled the restaurant's kitchen for a midnight snack, resulting in this style of salad, which Grauman then ordered again the next day. It became an overnight sensation.

SERVES 4–6

A DISNEY CLASSIC

FOR SALAD

1. Toss the iceberg lettuce, chicory, and watercress together, and arrange in a salad bowl.

2. In straight and separate lines, arrange the turkey, tomatoes, avocado, blue cheese, bacon, and eggs on top of the greens.

3. Sprinkle the chives in two diagonal lines across the salad.

4. To serve, present the salad at the table, toss with the dressing, and place on chilled plates with watercress sprigs as garnish.

SALAD

1 cup chopped iceberg lettuce leaves, washed and spun dry

1 cup chopped chicory leaves, washed and spun dry

1 cup tender sprigs watercress, washed and spun dry, plus additional sprigs for garnish

1 pound poached turkey breast, finely chopped

2 medium-size ripe tomatoes, peeled, seeded, and finely chopped

1 avocado, peeled, seeded, and finely chopped

½ cup crumbled blue cheese (about 2½ ounces)

6 bacon slices, cooked crisp, drained, and crumbled

3 hard-boiled eggs, peeled and finely chopped

2 tablespoons snipped fresh chives

½ cup Hollywood Brown Derby Old-fashioned French Dressing, chilled (recipe follows)

FOR DRESSING

1. Whisk together the water, red wine vinegar, lemon juice, Worcestershire sauce, salt, garlic, sugar, freshly ground pepper, and dry mustard in a small bowl until well blended.

2. Whisking constantly, add the vegetable oil and the olive oil in a slow steady stream until the dressing is emulsified.

3. Store covered and chilled until ready to serve. Whisk the dressing to blend just before serving.

DRESSING

2 tablespoons water

2 tablespoons red wine vinegar

1 tablespoon fresh lemon juice

½ teaspoon Worcestershire sauce

½ teaspoon salt, or to taste

½ teaspoon minced garlic

¼ teaspoon sugar

¼ teaspoon freshly ground pepper, or to taste

⅛ teaspoon dry English mustard

⅓ cup vegetable oil

2 tablespoons olive oil

SPACE MONKEY

SWEET ENDINGS AND DESSERTS

Sci-Fi Dine-In Theater Restaurant opened in 1991 as a re-creation of a classic 1950s drive-in theater, where guests sit in "parked convertibles" under an "evening sky," while the big screen plays trailers and clips from horror films and science fiction thrillers of the era, as well as the occasional bit of intermission animation.

SERVES 1   **COCKTAIL**

12 ounces chocolate milk shake

¾ ounce coconut rum

¾ ounce crème de banana liqueur

Put all ingredients in a blender and mix well. Serve in a tall glass.

KEY LIME PIE

Starring Rolls Café opened with the park on May 1, 1989, and remained a popular quick-service stop until 2017. It was known for its inviting pastry case of morning treats and individual-sized desserts, and some guests also remember its intimate outdoor patio area with umbrella-covered tables that offered a quiet spot to plan the day or take a lunch break.

MAKES ONE 9-INCH PIE   **LEFT THE MENU BUT NOT FORGOTTEN**

GRAHAM CRACKER CRUST

6 tablespoons melted butter

3 tablespoons sugar

1⅓ cups graham cracker crumbs

FILLING

2 cups sweetened condensed milk

¼ cup plus 2 tablespoons key lime juice

2 eggs

1 teaspoon vanilla

FOR CRUST

1 Preheat oven to 350°F. Stir together butter, sugar, and graham cracker crumbs in a medium bowl. Firmly press the mixture into a 9-inch pie pan.

2 Bake crust for 8 minutes. Cool slightly.

FOR FILLING

1 Whisk together sweetened condensed milk and key lime juice in a medium bowl. Whisk in eggs one at a time. Add vanilla and stir to combine.

2 Slowly pour filling into crust. Bake at 10 minutes or until set.

3 Refrigerate at least 3 hours before serving.

AMARETTO FLAN WITH WHITE CHOCOLATE WHIP

The Hollywood Brown Derby restaurant takes diners back to the Golden Age of Hollywood, with a fine-dining menu that includes rich desserts. A notable sweet course from past menus is this amaretto flan. With heavy cream, it is more like custard than a traditional flan, and the amaretto adds a subtle almond flavor.

SERVES 6   **LEFT THE MENU BUT NOT FORGOTTEN**

AMARETTO FLAN

1 extra-large egg

4 extra-large egg yolks

½ cup sugar

3 cups heavy cream

½ teaspoon vanilla extract

¼ teaspoon almond extract

2 tablespoons amaretto liqueur

FOR AMARETTO FLAN

1. Preheat oven to 300°F. Mix egg, egg yolks, and sugar in the bowl of an electric mixer on low speed for 1 minute, scraping sides of bowl, until combined.

2. Scald heavy cream in a medium saucepan over medium heat for 6 to 8 minutes. Do not boil.

3. Slowly add hot cream to eggs with mixer running on low speed.

4. Mix in vanilla extract, almond extract, and amaretto.

5. Pour custard into 6 (6-ounce) ramekins. Each ramekin should have ⅔ cup of custard.

6. Place ramekins in baking pan. Carefully pour boiling water into pan until it reaches halfway up sides of ramekin. Bake 35 to 40 minutes, until the flans are set when gently shaken.

7. Remove from oven and remove ramekins from water. Cool for 4 hours or until flans are room temperature. Refrigerate for 8 hours or until flan is firm.

THE HOLLYWOOD BROWN DERBY · HOLLYWOOD BOULEVARD

FOR WHITE CHOCOLATE WHIP

1. Heat heavy cream to boiling in a small saucepan over medium heat 2 to 3 minutes.

2. Remove from heat and add white chocolate chips, whisking constantly until melted.

3. Refrigerate for 8 to 24 hours.

TO SERVE

1. Whip cooled cream and white chocolate mixture in bowl of an electric mixer on high speed for 2 to 3 minutes, until soft peaks form.

2. Top each flan with 2 tablespoons of white chocolate whip and serve with amaretti cookies.

WHITE CHOCOLATE WHIP

1 cup heavy cream

½ cup white chocolate chips

GARNISH

6 amaretti cookies

Mickey, Minnie, and Pluto on a float in front of the Tree of Life, 2020

CHAPTER SEVEN
Disney's Animal Kingdom Theme Park and Nearby Resorts

ASIAN NOODLE SALAD

Since opening in 1998, Disney's Animal Kingdom Theme Park has entertained millions of guests through amazing adventures with wild and legendary animals, world-class stage shows and attractions, and diverse restaurants. This was the first Disney park to prominently showcase flavorful cuisine from Africa and India, giving many diners their first tastes of such foods. The quick-service restaurant Mr. Kamal's is a great example.

SERVES 4–6

SAVORY BITES

- 1 tablespoon canola oil
- 1 tablespoon peeled and minced fresh ginger
- 2 cloves garlic, peeled and minced
- ¼ cup sugar
- ¾ cup soy sauce
- ¼ cup water
- ¼ cup apple cider vinegar
- 2 tablespoons chili oil
- 1 pound dried spaghetti
- 2 tablespoons sesame oil, divided
- 1 ½ cups broccoli florets
- ¾ cup snow peas
- ¾ cup thinly sliced red pepper
- ¾ cup thinly sliced (matchstick) carrots
- ¼ cup green onion, thinly sliced on a diagonal
- 1 tablespoon black sesame seeds

1. Carefully heat oil in a large saucepan over medium heat. Add ginger and garlic and stir until fragrant, about 30 seconds.

2. Add sugar, soy sauce, water, apple cider vinegar, and chili oil, stirring well. Cook, stirring, until sugar melts and mixture simmers.

3. Meanwhile, cook spaghetti in a separate large pot of boiling water until just under al dente, about 5 minutes.

4. Drain noodles and, with caution, add to soy sauce dressing in saucepan; place over medium-low heat and toss with tongs until spaghetti absorbs dressing, about 5 minutes. Stir in 1 tablespoon sesame oil.

5. Remove from heat and spread noodles on a large baking sheet; place in freezer to chill quickly, but do not freeze.

6. Fill a large bowl about halfway with ice and water and set aside. Bring a large saucepan of water to a boil.

7 Blanch broccoli and snow peas in boiling water for 10 seconds, then transfer to ice water. After a few minutes, drain vegetables and pat dry.

8 Place cooked and cooled broccoli and snow peas, red pepper, and carrots in a large bowl; toss with remaining 1 tablespoon sesame oil.

9 Add cooled noodles to vegetables, tossing gently to thoroughly combine. Garnish with sliced green onions and black sesame seeds.

SAVANNA SPRING ROLLS

With the debut of Disney's Animal Kingdom Lodge in 2001, the Disney chefs had a big new playground for creating memorable dishes. Award-winning Jiko—The Cooking Place features African-inspired dishes paired with an impressive list of wines exclusively from Africa—one of the largest collections in any restaurant in the United States.

MAKES 8 SPRING ROLLS

SAVORY BITES

SPRING ROLLS

1 tablespoon olive oil

¼ cup diced yellow onion

1 teaspoon minced garlic

2 cups fresh corn

2 cups firmly packed mixed baby lettuce

½ teaspoon coarse salt

¼ teaspoon ground black pepper

½ cup soft goat cheese

4 (8-inch) square frozen spring roll pastry wrappers made with wheat flour, thawed

1 egg yolk, lightly beaten

vegetable oil for frying

FOR SPRING ROLLS

1 Carefully heat oil in a sauté pan over medium-high heat and add onions. Cook for 3 minutes, until softened, then add garlic; sauté 2 to 3 minutes.

2 Add corn and sauté 4 to 5 minutes, until corn is tender.

3 Add lettuce and cook 3 minutes, until wilted. Add salt and pepper. Set aside to cool for 5 minutes. Add goat cheese, and stir until well combined.

4 Cut wrappers in half diagonally, forming two triangles. With the long side of one triangle nearest you, put 2 tablespoons filling along middle of long edge of triangle, and shape filling into a thin log. Fold left and right corners of wrapper over filling, overlapping slightly. Dab top corner with egg yolk, then roll up wrapper away from you into a long thin roll, making sure ends and filling stay tucked inside. Place on a tray, seam side down. Repeat with remaining wrappers and filling, keeping tray of rolls loosely covered until ready to fry.

OPPOSITE, RIGHT: Rooms at Disney's Animal Kingdom Lodge are known for offering balcony views of thriving savannas, wildlife, and other impressive architectural details.

5 Heat 1½ inches of oil in a heavy-bottom stockpot over medium-high heat until it reaches 365°F. Working in batches, carefully fry rolls 4 to 5 minutes, until golden brown and crisp.

FOR CURRY VINAIGRETTE

1 Place oil, vinegar, lemon juice, sambal oelek, honey, garlic, and curry powder in a blender. Process until smooth.

2 Add dill, and stir to combine.

3 Serve as dipping sauce with spring rolls.

CURRY VINAIGRETTE

½ cup safflower oil

¼ cup rice vinegar

2 teaspoons lemon juice

2 teaspoons sambal oelek (Asian chili paste)

2 teaspoons honey

1 clove garlic, minced

¼ teaspoon curry powder

2 teaspoon finely chopped fresh dill

TOMATO FLORENTINE SOUP

Right next door to Jiko—The Cooking Place at Disney's Animal Kingdom Lodge, there's Boma—Flavors of Africa, where wood-burning grills create sensational aromas from morning until night in this marketplace-style restaurant. This slow-cooked stew is a family favorite.

SERVES 6

SAVORY BITES

2 tablespoons olive oil

1 pound ground turkey breast

1 teaspoon seasoning salt

¼ teaspoon freshly ground black pepper

½ cup diced carrots

½ cup diced celery

½ cup diced onion

1 tablespoon minced garlic

32 ounces chicken stock

28 ounces tomato sauce

2 cups finely diced fresh tomatoes

1 teaspoon Worcestershire sauce

1 dried bay leaf

½ teaspoon dried oregano

1 cup cooked elbow macaroni noodles

2 (6-ounce) bags baby spinach

1 Carefully heat oil in a large saucepan over medium heat. Add turkey, seasoning salt, and pepper. Cook, crumbling turkey into small pieces, 5 minutes, or until golden brown. Add carrots, celery, onions, and garlic. Cook until onions are translucent, about 3 minutes.

2 Stir in chicken stock, tomato sauce, diced tomatoes, Worchester, bay leaf, and oregano; simmer, covered, 30 minutes.

3 Add noodles and spinach just before serving, stirring to wilt spinach.

WATERMELON RIND SALAD

This bright salad was a favorite option at Boma—Flavors of Africa, where a half dozen side-by-side cooking stations feature curries, chutneys, and other Indian and Asian influences that add flavor to grilled fish, meat, and vegetables on the African-inspired menu.

4 pounds watermelon

1 cup thinly sliced ginger

½ cup sugar

1 cup rice vinegar

1 cup grenadine

1 cup water

MAKES 6 CUPS   **LEFT THE MENU BUT NOT FORGOTTEN**

FOR SALAD

1 Slice red fruit away from watermelon rind and skin. Scrub skin and scrape the white part of rind with a serrated spoon to remove most of red fruit.

2 Slice rind and skin into paper-thin strips with a mandoline. Set aside.

3 Stir together ginger, sugar, vinegar, grenadine, and water in a saucepan over medium-high heat. Reduce to a simmer and cook 10 minutes to let ginger infuse liquid. Remove from heat and slightly cool.

4 Stir in watermelon rind and marinate at least 1 hour. Refrigerate in an airtight container.

TO SERVE

Drain the rind and remove ginger slices.

NAAN BREAD WITH CUCUMBER RAITA

With a view of the resort's savanna from the cozy dining room, guests of Sanaa at Disney's Animal Kingdom Villas—Kidani Village are likely to see a giraffe or a zebra wander by the nine-foot windows as they dine on specialties such as aromatic curries, tandoori chicken, and naan bread.

SERVES 5

SAVORY BITES

NAAN BREAD

Makes 5 (8-inch) naan

3⅔ cups all-purpose flour

1 tablespoon sugar

1 tablespoon coarse salt

½ tablespoon baking soda

½ cup milk

⅔ cup warm water

1 tablespoon canola oil

4 tablespoons butter, melted

FOR BREAD

1. Combine flour, sugar, salt, and baking soda in the bowl of an electric mixer fitted with the paddle attachment; stir to combine.

2. Combine milk, water, and oil in a medium bowl; whisk to combine.

3. With mixer running, pour wet ingredients into dry ingredients. As soon as mixture comes together, switch attachment to a dough hook and mix until dough is smooth and no longer sticky. Do not over-mix.

4. Cover bowl with plastic wrap and set aside at room temperature for 1 hour.

5. Place a pizza stone on top rack of oven, positioned approximately 6 inches below the broiler. Preheat oven to 500°F for at least 30 minutes.

6. Divide dough evenly into 5 pieces. On a lightly floured surface, roll each piece into an 8-inch circle.

7 Turn oven to broil. Carefully slide one circle of dough onto the preheated pizza stone, and broil until bread is bubbled and golden brown, about 2 to 3 minutes. Watch carefully, as the bread can burn very quickly. Repeat with remaining dough rounds.

8 Brush the warm bread with melted butter and serve immediately.

FOR CUCUMBER RAITA

Combine all ingredients in medium bowl. Chill before serving.

CUCUMBER RAITA

Makes 2 cups

1 ½ cups Greek-style plain yogurt

1 cup cucumber, peeled, seeded, and diced into small pieces

½ small jalapeño pepper, seeds and stem removed, minced

½ teaspoon cumin seeds, toasted and freshly ground

⅛ teaspoon cayenne pepper

1 teaspoon coarse salt

LAMB KEFTA WITH TAMARIND SAUCE

At Disney's Animal Kingdom Villas—Kidani Village, Sanaa is a melting pot of vibrant tastes from the African islands of the Indian Ocean: Zanzibar, the Seychelles, the Comoro Islands, Mauritius, and Madagascar.

SERVES 6 AS AN APPETIZER   **LEFT THE MENU BUT NOT FORGOTTEN**

SAUCE

¼ teaspoon whole cloves

¼ teaspoon fennel seeds

¼ teaspoon cardamom pods

⅛ teaspoon red pepper flakes

⅛ teaspoon black peppercorns

1 ½ teaspoon coarse salt

¼ teaspoon cinnamon

2 tablespoons tamarind pulp (available at organic markets and ethnic grocery stores)

⅓ cup dark brown sugar

¼ cup lemon juice

1 tablespoon finely chopped garlic

1 tablespoon finely chopped fresh ginger

2 tablespoons cornstarch

2 tablespoons water

½ cup finely diced dried papaya

FOR SAUCE

1 Combine cloves, fennel seeds, cardamom pods, red pepper flakes, and black peppercorns in a medium nonstick skillet. Heat over medium-high heat, stirring constantly until spices become fragrant and the pan just begins to smoke. Remove from heat and immediately transfer spices to a plate to cool.

2 When cool, grind spices to a fine powder using a mortar and pestle or a spice grinder. Stir in salt and cinnamon.

3 Combine tamarind pulp, brown sugar, lemon juice, garlic, ginger, and spice mixture in a medium nonstick skillet. Cook over medium heat, whisking constantly until tamarind has softened and mixture is smooth and well combined, about 3 to 5 minutes.

4 Combine cornstarch and 2 tablespoons of water in a small bowl. Using a small whisk or a fork, stir until mixture is smooth and lumps have all dissolved. Add cornstarch mixture to tamarind mixture, whisking constantly until mixture is smooth. Continue to cook sauce over medium heat, stirring occasionally, until it has thickened and is glossy. It should be the consistency of honey.

(RECIPE CONTINUES ON PAGE 116)

5 Remove from heat, let cool slightly, and strain through a fine sieve.

6 Stir in diced papaya. If using immediately, cover and set aside. If not using immediately, let cool completely, then cover and refrigerate.

FOR KEFTA

1 Preheat oven to 375°F.

2 Combine cumin and black pepper in a medium nonstick skillet. Heat over medium-high heat, stirring constantly until spices become fragrant and the pan just begins to smoke. Remove from heat immediately and transfer spices to a plate to cool.

3 Combine toasted spices, paprika, cayenne, and salt. Mix well to combine.

4 In a large bowl, combine ground lamb, spice mixture, onion, garlic, mint, and parsley. Mix thoroughly until well combined.

5 Divide mixture into 18 portions and roll each portion into a ball. The Kefta should be about 2 inches in diameter.

6 In a large straight-sided skillet, heat canola oil over medium-high heat. When oil begins to simmer, add kefta, being careful not to overcrowd the pan. You will have to cook in 2 or 3 batches. Brown kefta on all sides, using tongs to turn as needed.

7 When completely browned, remove kefta to a rimmed baking sheet. Continue to cook remaining kefta in batches, until all have been browned.

KEFTA

Makes 18 (2-inch) meatballs

1 ½ teaspoons ground cumin

½ teaspoon freshly ground black pepper

1 teaspoon paprika

1 teaspoon cayenne pepper

1 tablespoon coarse salt

2 pounds ground lamb

¾ cup finely chopped onion

6 garlic cloves, finely chopped

¼ cup finely chopped fresh mint leaves

¼ cup finely chopped fresh Italian parsley

2 tablespoons canola or vegetable oil

6 sprigs of fresh mint, for garnish

8   Place baking sheet in oven and cook until kefta are firm, 5 to 7 minutes. Cut one kefta in half to determine doneness. It should be faintly pink to completely cooked through in the center.

9   Meanwhile, remove excess oil from skillet. Then add sauce to the skillet and cook over low heat, stirring occasionally and scraping the bottom of the skillet to incorporate all of the browned bits into the sauce.

10   When kefta are cooked to desired doneness, remove from oven and, using tongs, add to the skillet with the sauce. Stir gently to cover all of the kefta with the sauce. Simmer over low heat for 3 to 5 minutes.

SUGARCANE MOJITO

Dawa Bar is adjacent to the Tusker House Restaurant, where guests can try South African wines, African beers, and specialty cocktails.

SERVES 1   COCKTAIL

SUGARCANE SIMPLE SYRUP

1 cup turbinado sugar

1 cup water

MOJITO

2 ounces Starr African Rum

4 large fresh mint leaves

2 tablespoons simple syrup

2 lime wedges

Club soda, for serving

FOR SUGARCANE SIMPLE SYRUP

1 Combine sugar and water in a medium saucepan over medium-high heat. Bring to a boil.

2 Turn heat to low and stir constantly until sugar dissolves completely and mixture is clear, about 3 to 5 minutes.

FOR MOJITO

1 Combine rum, mint leaves, and simple syrup in a cocktail shaker filled with ice. Squeeze lime wedges into mixture and add to shaker. Cover shaker and shake vigorously 30 seconds.

2 Pour mixture into a tall glass and top with soda water.

MARINATED CABBAGE SLAW

At Jiko—The Cooking Place, the menu changes often, with bold flavors that heighten each dish: tastes like lime chakalaka, green mango atjar, and mitmita gremolata are hints of interesting cultures.

SERVES 6   **LEFT THE MENU BUT NOT FORGOTTEN**

1 cup white wine vinegar

⅓ cup sugar

1 teaspoon celery seed

2 teaspoons caraway seed

1 teaspoon sambal oelek (Asian chili paste)

½ head of cabbage, thinly shredded

1 cup shredded carrots, about 4 large

1 cup thinly sliced red onion

1 Bring vinegar to a boil in a small saucepan. Add sugar, celery seed, caraway seed, and sambal oelek. Simmer about 10 minutes, then cool.

2 In a large mixing bowl, stir together cabbage, carrot, and red onion.

3 Stir in liquid and marinate at least 8 hours before serving. Best if marinated 24 hours.

SPICY DURBAN-STYLE CHICKEN

MAINS AND SIDES

Across the three signature restaurants (Sanaa, Boma—Flavors of Africa, and Jiko—The Cooking Place), gracious hosts are part of Disney's Cultural Representative Program, sharing stories of their homelands with guests. Every meal is like a trip around the world, no passport required.

Increase the spiciness of this dish by adding additional jalapeños and chili powder. Cardamom pods can be found in Indian grocery stores. Some stores call them seeds rather than pods. Each pod is about the size of a dried cranberry and contains seventeen to twenty tiny seeds.

SERVES 4   **LEFT THE MENU BUT NOT FORGOTTEN**

FOR DRY MASALA

1 Toast star anise, cumin seeds, bay leaves, and cardamom pods in a heavy, dry skillet over medium heat 3 to 4 minutes, stirring until spices begin to brown and are fragrant. Remove from heat and cool.

2 Grind spices in a blender or a coffee grinder into a fine powder.

3 Combine spice mixture with cinnamon, chili powder, ancho chili powder, Madras curry powder, and turmeric powder. Toast in heavy, dry skillet over medium heat 1 to 2 minutes, stirring until fragrant. Remove from skillet and set aside to cool.

DRY MASALA

1 whole star anise

½ tablespoon whole cumin seeds

2 whole bay leaves

4 green cardamon pods

1 teaspoon fresh ground cinnamon

1 ½ tablespoons chili powder

1 ½ tablespoons ancho chili powder

1 ½ tablespoons Madras curry powder

2 teaspoons turmeric powder

CHICKEN AND CURRY SAUCE

¼ cup canola oil

1 ¼ pounds boneless, skinless chicken thighs

coarse salt, to taste

freshly ground black pepper, to taste

FOR CHICKEN AND CURRY SAUCE

1 Carefully heat oil in a large heavy skillet over medium heat. Trim fat from chicken and cut into 1-inch cubes. Season with salt and pepper. Place chicken in skillet and brown 8 to 10 minutes, turning to evenly cook. Remove from skillet and set aside.

2 Add onions and jalapeños to skillet and cook 4 to 5 minutes, or until onions are translucent. Add ginger and garlic, stirring to combine. Cook 1 minute. Mix in dry masala mixture with a rubber spatula and cook 1 minute,

3 Stir in tomatoes and increase heat to high for 3 to 4 minutes.

4 Return chicken to skillet, add water, and stir to combine. Bring mixture to a boil, reduce heat to low, and simmer 10 to 12 minutes, or until sauce slightly thickens. Stir in cilantro. Serve immediately over basmati rice.

1 cup diced yellow onion

2 jalapeño peppers, seeded and minced

1 tablespoon grated fresh ginger

1 tablespoon minced fresh garlic

3 cups canned crushed tomatoes with juice

1½ cups water

¼ cup minced cilantro

4 cups cooked balsamic rice, for serving

SANAA · DISNEY'S ANIMAL KINGDOM VILLAS—KIDANI VILLAGE

PERI PERI SALMON

Disney guests are well traveled and love exploring new tastes, and each new restaurant reflects our chefs' desires to surprise and delight diners. *Peri peri*, or *piripiri*, is the Swahili word for "pepper pepper." Sambal is a hot sauce typically made from a variety of chili peppers and other ingredients, like garlic, ginger, lime juice, vinegar, shrimp paste, and/or fish sauce. It can usually be found in the international food aisle of the grocery store.

SERVES 6

LEFT THE MENU BUT NOT FORGOTTEN

FOR SALMON

1. Whisk together sambal, oil, paprika, crab seasoning, Italian seasoning, salt, and pepper in a small bowl.

2. Coat salmon in mixture; place in a shallow dish, cover tightly with plastic wrap, and refrigerate 2 hours.

3. Preheat oven to 350°F. Carefully heat oil mixture in a large nonstick skillet over high heat. Sear salmon in skillet until golden, about 2 minutes. Flip, then place skillet in oven and cook 3 to 5 minutes, or until fish is cooked through.

FOR SPICY TOMATO TOPPING

1. Combine all ingredients in a small bowl.

2. Spoon over salmon just before serving.

PERI PERI SALMON

¼ cup sambal chili sauce

1 tablespoon olive oil

1 tablespoon paprika

1 teaspoon crab seasoning, such as Old Bay

1 teaspoon Italian seasoning

½ teaspoon coarse salt

¼ teaspoon freshly ground black pepper

4 (6-ounce) salmon filets

SPICY TOMATO TOPPING

1 large tomato, finely diced

2 cloves garlic, finely minced

¼ cup extra-virgin olive oil

2 tablespoons sambal chili sauce

2 tablespoons chopped fresh basil

½ teaspoon coarse salt

¼ teaspoon freshly ground black pepper

CHICKPEA SALAD

Tamarind paste has a distinctive, tart flavor. It can be purchased in Asian and Latin American grocery stores or online. Chaat masala is a spice blend available in specialty food stores and some grocery stores or online.

SERVES 8 AS A SIDE DISH OR AN APPETIZER

LEFT THE MENU BUT NOT FORGOTTEN

2 tablespoons olive oil

1 tablespoon minced garlic

1 tablespoon minced fresh ginger

½ small jalapeño pepper, seeds removed, minced

1 teaspoon tamarind paste, dissolved in 3 tablespoons water

¼ teaspoon chaat masala, optional

½ medium yellow onion, diced

2 (14.5-ounce) cans chickpeas, drained and rinsed

2 to 3 tablespoons fresh lime juice, divided

coarse salt, to taste

freshly ground black pepper, to taste

½ cucumber, peeled, seeded, and diced

1 large tomato, seeds removed, diced

½ bunch cilantro, stems removed, minced

1 Carefully heat oil in a small sauté pan over medium heat. Add garlic, ginger, and jalapeño; cook until garlic is light gold. Set aside until mixture is room temperature. Whisk in tamarind paste and chaat masala. Stir in onion. Refrigerate until cold.

2 Add chilled spice mixture to chickpeas, tossing to coat. Add 2 tablespoons lime juice, stirring to combine. Season with salt and pepper. Refrigerate at least 1 hour.

3 Just before serving, add cucumber, tomato, and cilantro. Add remaining lime juice, if desired. Serve chilled or at room temperature.

FLAME TREE BARBECUE SAUCE

Flame Tree Barbecue is a quick-service restaurant that debuted on the opening day of Disney's Animal Kingdom Theme Park: April 22, 1998, which was that year's Earth Day. It quickly became one of the most popular spots for barbecue throughout the Walt Disney World Resort.

MAKES 1 CUP

A DISNEY CLASSIC

1 cup ketchup

¼ cup rice wine vinegar

2 tablespoons molasses

1 tablespoon chili powder

1 tablespoon paprika

1 teaspoon ground turmeric

1 teaspoon ground cumin

½ teaspoon garlic powder

½ teaspoon ground cloves

2 teaspoons onion powder

⅔ cup water

¼ cup packed light brown sugar

1 tablespoon Worcestershire sauce

½ teaspoon salt

1 Combine all ingredients in a medium saucepan over medium heat. Bring to a simmer, reduce heat to low, and cook for 25 minutes, stirring frequently.

2 Use immediately or store in refrigerator for up to 2 weeks.

FLAME TREE BARBECUE · DISCOVERY ISLAND, DISNEY'S ANIMAL KINGDOM THEME PARK

FLAME TREE BARBECUE RUB

As outdoor dining options go, Flame Tree Barbecue offers something truly special. Numerous patio coverings with whimsical and colorful carvings are surrounded by lush gardens—all themed to relationships in the great circle of life. Imagineers designed each seating area with a unique artistic representation of a hunter and a hunted, such as snakes slithering after mice; spiders spinning after butterflies; and owls preying on rabbits. The motif even extends to the tables and chairs: the diner is seated on a chair representing a predator, while the table is adorned with prey animals.

1 cup sugar

¼ cup Lawry's seasoning salt

2 tablespoons paprika

2 tablespoons chili powder

2 tablespoons black pepper

2 tablespoons cumin

2 teaspoons garlic salt

2 teaspoons onion powder

MAKES 2 CUPS

A DISNEY CLASSIC

Mix all ingredients and apply to meat 2 to 3 hours before cooking. Do not leave rub on overnight; it will dry out the meat.

MANGO LASSI

If you can't be at Disney's Animal Kingdom Villas—Kidani Village, this bright drink will help you share a vacation-dining experience at home with your friends and family.

SERVES 4

MOCKTAIL

2 cups ripe mango, chopped

1 pinch salt

1 cup chilled whole milk

1 cup whole-milk plain yogurt

2 to 3 teaspoons sugar, optional

1   If mango has stringy fibers, push through a nylon sieve with the back of a spoon. Remaining mango should not contain any stringy pulp. Refrigerate until cold.

2   Combine mango, salt, milk, and yogurt in a blender and puree until smooth. Add sugar if using it. If you would like lassi a bit colder, add ice to blender. Can be refrigerated up to 24 hours.

SANAA · DISNEY'S ANIMAL KINGDOM VILLAS—KIDANI VILLAGE

FRUNCH

After a special meal at home, this refreshing punch will remind you of a dinner at Boma—Flavors of Africa, where guests can take a stroll alongside the resort's own savanna with wildebeests, zebras, giraffes, and more African animals.

MAKES 12 CUPS　　　　　　　　　　**COCKTAIL**

2 cups mango nectar

1 (12-ounce) can frozen pineapple concentrate, thawed

1 (12-ounce) can lemonade concentrate, thawed

2 cups fresh orange juice

5 cups water

¼ cup grenadine

Mix all ingredients together in a 1-gallon pitcher. Serve over ice in tall glasses.

AFRICAN FRUIT FOOL

To cube a mango for this dessert, cut off a "cheek" (roundish side) with a paring knife. Start by gently making parallel cuts down to the skin, but do not cut through the skin. Repeat the process going the other direction until you have a grid. Put down the knife, pick up the mango, and with both hands push up on the skin underneath to invert the mango. Slide the knife along the skin to free the cubes.

SERVES 6   **GREAT FOR KIDS**

1 cup diced fresh pineapple

1 green apple, peeled and diced

1 small ripe mango, peeled and diced (about 1 cup)

1 cup diced fresh papaya

2 cups red seedless grapes

3 bananas, peeled and sliced

1 cup shredded coconut

¾ cup sweetened condensed milk

1 cup cream, well chilled

1 teaspoon vanilla extract

1 Combine pineapple, apple, mango, papaya, grapes, bananas, and coconut in a large bowl. Gently stir to combine. Stir in sweetened condensed milk.

2 Whip cream until soft peaks form. Add vanilla and continue to beat just until soft peaks form. Working in batches, gently fold whipped cream into fruit mixture.

3 Cover bowl with plastic wrap. Refrigerate until cold, about 30 minutes.

CHAI CREAM

For this creamy creation, use a cheese grater or a vegetable peeler to shave semisweet chocolate from a solid bar.

SERVES 8

GREAT FOR KIDS

5⅓ plus ½ cups heavy whipping cream

1 vanilla bean, split lengthwise and scraped, seeds reserved

1 cup sugar

1-ounce envelope powdered gelatin

2 teaspoons black chai tea, ground in a coffee or spice grinder

1 cinnamon stick

6 green cardamom pods

6 whole black peppercorns

1 tablespoon powdered sugar

1 tablespoon semisweet chocolate shavings

1 Combine 5 cups of cream, vanilla bean seeds, and sugar in a medium saucepan over medium-high heat. Bring to a simmer, stirring occasionally.

2 Place ⅓ cup cream in a small bowl and add powdered gelatin. Stir to mix.

3 When cream-sugar mixture comes to a simmer, immediately remove from heat and add cream-gelatin mixture, stirring well until gelatin is completely dissolved. Add tea, cinnamon, cardamom pods, and peppercorns.

4 Let mixture steep for 10 minutes, stirring occasionally. Pour mixture into a metal bowl set in a larger bowl of ice water. Cover with plastic wrap, and let steep and cool for 30 minutes.

5 Pour mixture through a fine-mesh sieve into a clean bowl. Freeze for 20 minutes, or until mixture starts to thicken. (This additional cooling allows gelatin to set slightly so specks of tea remain in suspension instead of falling to bottom of glasses.)

6 Divide mixture evenly among 8 (5-ounce) glasses or ramekins, and refrigerate for at least 4 hours before serving. Before serving, combine remaining ½ cup cream and powdered sugar in a large bowl. Whip with an electric mixer until stiff peaks form. Dollop whipped cream onto each glass, then sprinkle with semisweet chocolate shavings. Serve immediately.

STONE FRUIT SAMOSAS

Samosas are a traditional Indian pastry, and this recipe is inspired by the seasonal fruit samosas that were served at Sanaa, where the menu features African cooking with Indian flavors. It was originally deep-fried, but we've created a baked version made with phyllo.

MAKES 12 SAMOSAS   **LEFT THE MENU BUT NOT FORGOTTEN**

SAMOSAS

1 ½ cups diced peaches

2 teaspoons sugar

½ teaspoon ground cinnamon

2 teaspoons cornstarch

36 (3×8-inch) strips of thawed phyllo dough

¼ cup butter, melted

FRUIT SALSA

½ cup diced peaches

½ cup diced mango

1 tablespoon diced crystallized ginger

1 tablespoon diced cherries

FOR SAMOSAS

1 Preheat oven to 350°F. Line a baking sheet with parchment paper.

2 Mix peaches, sugar, cinnamon, and cornstarch in a medium bowl.

3 Place 3 strips of phyllo on top of each other on a floured breadboard. Cover remaining strips with plastic wrap and a damp kitchen towel.

4 Gently brush top strip with butter. Put 1 tablespoon of peach mixture near bottom left corner and fold corner of phyllo strips over to enclose filling and form a triangle. Continue folding strips, maintaining triangle shape.

5 Seal by brushing with butter. Repeat with remining phyllo strips and peach mixture.

6 Bake for 20 to 25 minutes, until golden brown.

FOR FRUIT SALSA

1 Mix diced peaches, mango, and crystallized ginger in a small bowl.

2 Before serving, add diced cherries.

3 Serve with warm samosas.

D-Luxe Burger at Disney Springs, 2016

CHAPTER EIGHT
Across the Walt Disney World Resort

HONEY-CORIANDER CHICKEN WINGS

'Ohana is one of the two flagship restaurants on the second floor of the Great Ceremonial House of Disney's Polynesian Village Resort. The open dining room is framed by large windows looking out onto the resort's gardens and boat marina below and is set around an eighteen-foot semicircular firepit, where guests can watch food being grilled.

SERVES 4–6

SAVORY BITES

FOR CORIANDER CHICKEN WINGS

1. Preheat oven to 500°F, with racks in upper and lower thirds. Line two rimmed baking sheets with foil and spray with nonstick cooking spray.

2. Combine all ingredients except chicken in large glass bowl. Stir to combine. Add chicken and toss to coat.

3. Divide chicken in single layer between prepared baking sheets and bake until browned and completely cooked through, about 35 minutes, rotating baking sheets on racks and turning chicken halfway through cooking.

FOR WING SAUCE

1. While wings are baking, combine ingredients in small saucepan over medium-high heat. Bring to boil, stirring occasionally, until liquid thickens and reduces to a syrup, about 5 minutes. Remove from heat and cool 10 minutes.

2. Brush or toss baked chicken with wing sauce to coat. Serve with remaining wing sauce on the side or with preferred dipping sauce.

CORIANDER CHICKEN WINGS

1 tablespoon coarse salt

2 tablespoons paprika

2 tablespoons sugar

½ teaspoon black pepper

½ teaspoon turmeric

½ teaspoon ground cinnamon

¼ teaspoon cayenne pepper

4 tablespoons canola oil

4 pounds chicken wings or drumettes, patted dry

HONEY WING SAUCE

1 tablespoon chili powder

½ teaspoon ground ginger

1 tablespoon ground coriander

2 tablespoons lime juice

½ cup soy sauce

1 cup honey

¾ cup water

2 tablespoons cornstarch

KONA SALAD

This signature salad is from Kona Café, the other of the two flagship restaurants on the second floor of the Great Ceremonial House at Disney's Polynesian Village Resort. The dishes here are classic American cuisine infused with some Asian influences. If Asian pears are not available, you can substitute fresh peaches, strawberries, or other berries—whatever is in season.

SERVES 8

A DISNEY CLASSIC

3 unpeeled Asian pears, cored and thinly sliced

9 cups (or 1-pound bag) spring mix or gourmet lettuce mix

1 cup crumbled blue cheese

¼ cup thinly sliced red onion

¾ cup smoked almonds, chopped in large pieces

6 tablespoons fresh-squeezed orange juice

2 tablespoons rice vinegar

1 teaspoon granulated sugar

½ cup canola oil

¼ teaspoon coarse salt

⅛ teaspoon freshly ground black pepper

1 In a large bowl, gently toss pears, salad mix, blue cheese, onion, and almonds.

2 In a separate bowl, mix orange juice, rice vinegar, and sugar. Whisk in canola oil, salt, and pepper.

3 Pour over salad and gently toss; serve immediately.

CLASSIC SCONES

For your traditional afternoon tea party, let the star of your menu be this British-inspired scone from the Garden View Tea Room on the first floor of the main lobby building at Disney's Grand Floridian Resort & Spa. For a sweeter treat, sprinkle granulated sugar on top of the scones before baking.

MAKES 40 (2-INCH) SCONES   **A DISNEY CLASSIC**

4 cups all-purpose flour

3 tablespoons baking powder

½ cup sugar

1 teaspoon salt

2 tablespoons margarine

2 tablespoons shortening

3 eggs, beaten

1 ¼ cups milk

1 cup golden raisins

1. Preheat oven to 425°F. Sift the flour, baking powder, sugar, and salt into a large mixing bowl. Work the margarine and shortening into the flour with fingertips until the mixture resembles coarse meal.

2. Combine the beaten eggs and milk in a separate bowl. Stir into the flour mixture just until the dough comes together. Fold in the raisins.

3. On a lightly floured surface, roll the dough out to about ½-inch thickness. With a 2-inch round cutter, cut out 40 scones and transfer them to a lightly greased baking sheet. Bake the scones for 12 to 15 minutes or until they are light brown. Serve at once with Devonshire cream or butter and jam.

SMOKED-SALMON-AND-HERB MUFFINS

Another scrumptious snack, for teatime or celebrations, comes from one of the most popular conference and event spaces at the Walt Disney World Resort, the lakeside Disney's Coronado Springs Resort. It boasts nearly 228,000 square feet of indoor and outdoor function space, and the resort's catering program is at the ready with a variety of food and beverages for all meals of the day.

MAKES 24 MINI MUFFINS

SAVORY BITES

1 ¼ cups all-purpose flour

1 tablespoon baking powder

¼ teaspoon salt

¼ teaspoon ground pepper

1 cup mayonnaise

1 egg, beaten

½ cup plus 1 tablespoon melted butter

1 cup milk

2 tablespoons chopped fresh dill

2 tablespoons chopped fresh chives

½ cup cream cheese

2 tablespoons capers

12 thin slices smoked salmon

fresh dill sprigs

1 Preheat oven to 400°F. Spray mini-muffin tins with nonstick spray.

2 Stir together flour, baking powder, salt, and pepper in a large bowl.

3 In a separate bowl, whisk together mayonnaise, egg, melted butter, and milk. Stir in dill and chives.

4 Pour milk mixture into flour mixture and stir until just combined.

5 Fill muffin tins three-quarters full with batter. Bake 25 to 35 minutes, until golden. Transfer to wire rack to cool.

6 Combine cream cheese and capers. Cut muffins in half widthwise. Spread each half with cream cheese mixture, top with a folded slice of smoked salmon, and top that with dill sprig, then sandwich together. Serve at room temperature.

BIG APPLE SUNSET

With the exception of a few weeks, the Walt Disney World Resort has festivals year-round, each offering exceptional food and drink. (See CHAPTER FIVE: EPCOT for some notable highlights.) Then there is the regular Walt Disney World bar menu, which offers specialty cocktails bartenders across the property know well and can make uniformly. The fruity delights on this and the next page come from that menu.

1 ¼ ounces Van Gogh Wild Apple Vodka

¾ ounce sour apple schnapps

½ ounce sour mix

¼ ounce Chambord Raspberry Liqueur

Apple slices, for garnish

SERVES 1

COCKTAIL

In a shaker with ice, mix vodka, schnapps, and sour mix. Strain. Finish with Chambord. (Do not stir.) Serve in a chilled martini glass garnished with apple slices.

WATERMELON MIST

This delicious icy concoction is worthy of a party!

SERVES 1

COCKTAIL

Blend the first four ingredients with just enough ice to make a loose slush. Pour into a martini glass and garnish with a wedge of watermelon and fresh mint.

1 ¼ ounces watermelon schnapps

¾ ounce Midori

2 ounces cranberry juice

Crushed ice

Watermelon wedge, for garnish

Fresh mint, for garnish

PINK LEILANI

This vintage cocktail hails from the Coral Isle Café, which debuted on the second floor of the Great Ceremonial House of Disney's Polynesian Village Resort when the Walt Disney World Resort premiered October 1, 1971. The menu—and the physical space—has evolved through the years. Today we know it as Kona Café.

SERVES 1

COCKTAIL

2 cups fresh strawberries (frozen may be substituted)

3 cups orange juice

1 tablespoon grenadine

Orange slice, for garnish

Fresh strawberry, for garnish

1 Puree strawberries in a blender. Add orange juice and grenadine.

2 Serve in a tall glass over crushed ice, with orange and strawberry garnish.

HOOPLA

The Adventurers Club debuted as an immersive nightclub along with the opening of Pleasure Island in 1989 and notably ran operations until the entire Pleasure Island area closed in 2008 to make way for the Disney Springs project. Throughout nearly two decades, the nightclub picked up a devoted fan base that relished in the club's surprises and curious artifacts that, as its legend went, were accumulated by Merriweather Adam Pleasure's adventures around the world.

¾ ounce coconut rum

½ ounce vodka

¾ ounce melon liqueur

6 ounces pineapple juice

SERVES 1 **COCKTAIL**

In a cocktail shaker, mix all ingredients. Serve in a cocktail glass over ice.

CHARDONNAY STEAMED PENN COVE MUSSELS WITH PESTO CREAM SAUCE

Flying Fish at Disney's BoardWalk Inn and Villas is stylish at every turn, from subtle and elegant sea-inspired décor to mouthwatering menu options. Basil pesto, in the recipe, is a blend of fresh basil, olive oil, garlic, pine nuts, and Parmesan cheese that can be found in most grocery stores and specialty stores.

SERVES 6-8   **LEFT THE MENU BUT NOT FORGOTTEN**

1 Simmer cream in 4-quart saucepan over medium-low heat for 12 to 15 minutes, or until reduced by half. Stir in basil pesto.

2 Heat olive oil in 12-quart stockpot over medium heat. Add shallots and garlic, and sauté 1 to 2 minutes or until tender. Add red pepper flakes and fennel, continuing to sauté for 2 to 3 minutes or until fennel is tender.

3 Add mussels, then Chardonnay. Cover and cook 10 to 12 minutes, or until mussels open. Discard any unopened mussels.

4 Gently mix in reduced cream and cook for 2 minutes. Season to taste with salt and pepper. Serve immediately.

2 quarts heavy whipping cream

¾ cup basil pesto

4 tablespoons olive oil

3 medium shallots, thinly sliced

12 cloves garlic, minced

1 teaspoon red pepper flakes

1 fennel bulb, thinly sliced

4 pounds Penn Cove mussels (any variety can be substituted)

1 cup Chardonnay

coarse salt, to taste

freshly ground black pepper, to taste

GROUPER WITH ASIAN VEGETABLES, STICKY RICE, AND GINGER-SOY BROTH

California Grill features a lively onstage kitchen where guests can hear the sounds and catch a glimpse of meals being prepared. Food offerings at this location draw inspiration from California to highlight fresh seasonal ingredients and various combinations of international cuisine elements.

SERVES 4   **LEFT THE MENU BUT NOT FORGOTTEN**

FOR GINGER-SOY BROTH

1 Combine olive oil, shallots, ginger, garlic, and jalapeño in a medium saucepan. Cook over medium-high heat, stirring occasionally, until mixture begins to soften, about 5 minutes.

2 Add the lemongrass and reduce heat to medium. Cook, stirring occasionally, for 5 minutes longer.

3 Add remaining ingredients and reduce heat to low. Cook for 5 minutes, stirring occasionally.

4 Remove from heat and cover. Let sit for 40 minutes. Strain and set aside until ready to serve

FOR SUSHI RICE

1 Cook rice according to package directions.

2 Combine vinegar, sugar, and salt in a small saucepan. Cook over high heat, stirring constantly, until sugar and salt dissolve.

GINGER-SOY BROTH

2 tablespoons extra-virgin olive oil

3 shallots, peeled and finely chopped

1 (2-inch) piece ginger, peeled and finely chopped

1 clove garlic, peeled and finely chopped

1 jalapeño, seeds removed, finely chopped

1½ tablespoons finely chopped lemongrass

1½ teaspoons sesame oil

1 cup chicken stock

2 tablespoons rice vinegar

2 tablespoons tamari

⅓ cup low-sodium soy sauce

2 tablespoons mirin

1 tablespoon Vietnamese fish sauce

1 tablespoon sweet soy sauce

SUSHI RICE

1 cup uncooked sushi rice

¼ cup rice wine vinegar

1½ tablespoons sugar

1 teaspoon coarse salt

3 Remove from heat and pour over cooked rice, mixing until completely coated. Cover and set aside

FOR STIR-FRY SAUCE

1 Whisk together all ingredients in a medium bowl.

2 Cover and set aside until ready to use.

FOR GROUPER

1 Preheat oven to 400°F. Pat the fish fillets dry with a paper towel, and season well on both sides with salt and pepper. Set aside.

2 Combine hijiki and 2 tablespoons of water in a small bowl. Let soak for 30 minutes, then drain, discarding water. Set aside.

(RECIPE CONTINUES ON PAGE 152)

STIR-FRY SAUCE

1 tablespoon Vietnamese fish sauce

2 tablespoons rice wine vinegar

1 ½ tablespoons sweet soy sauce

2 tablespoons soy sauce

1 tablespoon sesame oil

2 tablespoons extra-virgin olive oil

1 teaspoon finely chopped garlic

1 teaspoon finely chopped ginger

1 tablespoon sambal oelek (hot chili paste)

1 tablespoon sugar

¼ teaspoon coarse salt

GROUPER WITH ASIAN VEGETABLES, STICKY RICE, AND GINGER-SOY BROTH

(CONTINUED)

3 Warm the ginger-soy broth in a small saucepan over medium heat. Keep warm until ready to serve.

4 Heat 2 tablespoons of olive oil over medium-high heat in a medium skillet. Add the carrots, red onion, and green beans. Cook, stirring constantly, for 3 minutes.

5 With caution, add the stir-fry sauce to the pan and bring to a boil. Remove from the heat.

6 Add the green papaya, stir to coat all of the vegetables with the sauce, and set aside.

7 Heat remaining 2 tablespoons of olive oil over medium-high heat in a medium skillet. Once oil is very hot and begins to simmer, add the fish fillets to the pan using tongs.

8 Cook for 5 minutes on both sides. Remove fillets to a baking sheet and place in oven for an additional 5 to 7 minutes or until very firm to the touch.

TO SERVE

1 Divide rice into four bowls.

2 Sprinkle rice with cilantro, mint, and hijiki.

3 Divide stir-fry vegetables and sauce between the bowls.

4 Place fish on top of vegetables and pour ginger-soy sauce over fish. Serve immediately.

GROUPER

4 (6-ounce) black grouper fillets, boneless, skin removed (halibut or red snapper can be substituted)

coarse salt, to taste

freshly ground black pepper, to taste

2 tablespoons hijiki seaweed (arame can be substituted)

¼ cup extra-virgin olive oil

1 carrot, peeled and cut into 2-inch matchsticks

½ red onion, very thinly sliced

1 cup green beans, trimmed and cut into 2-inch pieces

1 small green papaya, peeled and cut into 2-inch matchsticks (cucumber may be substituted)

1 tablespoon finely chopped cilantro, for serving

1 tablespoon finely chopped mint, for serving

CHEF MICKEY'S BREAKFAST PIZZA

This kid-pleasing dish is a great way to recall the good times at one of the most celebratory character dining experiences across the World Disney World Resort: Chef Mickey's.

SERVES 6　　　　　　　　　　**GREAT FOR KIDS**

1 (12-inch) Boboli pizza crust or other precooked pizza shell

½ cup coarsely grated mozzarella cheese

½ cup coarsely grated provolone cheese

1 cup coarsely grated cheddar cheese

2 large eggs

¼ cup heavy cream

coarse salt, to taste

freshly ground pepper, to taste

1. Preheat oven to 375°F. Place pizza crust on a baking sheet.

2. Blend the mozzarella, provolone, and cheddar cheeses in a medium bowl.

3. Beat together eggs and heavy cream in a small bowl with a fork. Season with salt and pepper. Add the cheese mixture to the egg mixture.

4. Immediately, to avoid clumping, transfer the cheese mixture to the pizza shell.

5. Bake for 10 to 12 minutes, or until the cheese mixture is set and beginning to brown.

6. Serve hot, cut into wedges.

GRILLED PORK TENDERLOIN

The award-winning California Grill on the fifteenth floor of Disney's Contemporary Resort showcases flavors of the Pacific Coast along with unparalleled panoramic views around Seven Seas Lagoon and Bay Lake.

To use this seasoned butter as a sauce for other grilled meats, fish, or poultry, roll it in a sheet of waxed paper, freeze it, and then cut into thin slices to top hot food; you'll have an instant sauce.

SERVES 4   **LEFT THE MENU BUT NOT FORGOTTEN**

MUSTARD BUTTER

6 tablespoons butter, softened

2 tablespoons Dijon mustard, at room temperature

2 tablespoons whole grain mustard (such as Pommery), at room temperature

2 teaspoons fresh lemon juice

1 teaspoon Worchester sauce

⅛ teaspoon freshly ground pepper, or to taste

PORK TENDERLOIN

6 tablespoons olive oil, divided

20 fresh sage leaves with stems, divided

½ teaspoon salt, or to taste

¼ teaspoon freshly ground pepper, or to taste

1 pound pork tenderloin, trimmed (reserve trimmings)

FOR MUSTARD BUTTER

1 In a small bowl, with a fork, combine all ingredients.

2 Can be covered and kept in refrigerator for up to two weeks.

FOR PORK TENDERLOIN

1 Carefully heat 4 tablespoons of the olive oil over medium-high heat in a 10-inch skillet until hot, but not smoking. With caution, add 5 of the sage leaves. Turn quickly, cooking for only 10 seconds. Immediately, with a slotted spoon, transfer the sage leaves to paper towels to drain. Repeat with remaining sage leaves. Set aside at room temperature until ready to serve.

2 Stir together the remaining 2 tablespoons of the olive oil, salt, and pepper on a plate. Completely coat the pork tenderloin with the olive oil mixture.

3 Preheat an empty 10-inch cast iron skillet over medium-high heat until very hot. Add the pork and sear, turning with tongs to brown all sides. Reduce the heat to medium and cook, turning frequently and basting occasionally with the mustard butter, for about 15 minutes, or just until the pork is cooked through. Set the pork aside, covered, on a cutting board, for 5 minutes to let the juices settle.

FOR ROASTED GARLIC PUREE

1 Preheat oven to 400°F. Cut off the stem and the top third of the garlic head. Place the garlic on a sheet of heavy-duty aluminum foil and drizzle with the olive oil. Wrap the garlic in foil, seal the edges tightly, and roast in the preheated 400°F oven for 1 hour.

2 Remove package from the oven, open carefully, and let the garlic cool slightly.

3 Scrape or squeeze out pulp from the garlic cloves, about 2 tablespoons roasted garlic puree from one head of garlic.

(RECIPE CONTINUES ON PAGE 156)

ROASTED GARLIC PUREE

1 whole garlic head

1 tablespoon olive oil

CALIFORNIA GRILL · DISNEY'S CONTEMPORARY RESORT

GRILLED PORK TENDERLOIN

(CONTINUED)

FOR GARLIC AND HERB POLENTA

1 Heat the olive oil over medium heat until hot, but not smoking, in a 3-quart saucepan. Add the onions and cook, stirring, for 3 minutes, or until softened. Stir in the roasted garlic puree. Add the water, milk, and heavy cream; bring the mixture to a simmer over high heat.

2 Add cornmeal in a slow steady stream, whisking constantly. Stir in the salt and pepper. Cook, stirring constantly, 15 to 20 minutes, or until thick and bubbling. Remove the saucepan from the heat and stir in the Asiago, goat cheese, thyme, and sage.

3 Serve the polenta hot, garnished with the parsley.

FOR ZINFANDEL GLAZE

1 Cook the wine and the onion over high heat for about 4 to 5 minutes in a 2-quart saucepan, or until liquid is reduced by half.

2 Add the broth, mushrooms, thyme, and peppercorns; reduce the liquid to about 1½ cups.

3 Meanwhile, set a 10-inch skillet over medium heat and add the meat trimmings and flour. Cook, stirring regularly, for about 3 minutes, or until trimmings are lightly browned.

4 Slowly whisk in the reduced wine mixture; cook, stirring, for 2 to 3 minutes, or until the mixture boils and thickens.

5 Strain the sauce through a fine sieve into a clean 1-quart saucepan. Discard the solids. Use immediately or store, covered and chilled, for up to one week.

GARLIC AND HERB POLENTA

1 tablespoon olive oil

½ cup finely chopped onion

2 teaspoons roasted garlic puree

1¼ cups water

1¼ cups milk

⅓ cup heavy cream

½ cup yellow cornmeal

½ teaspoon salt, or to taste

⅛ teaspoon freshly ground pepper, or to taste

2 tablespoons grated Asiago or Parmesan cheese

¼ cup crumbled soft mild goat cheese (such as Montrachet)

1 tablespoon minced fresh thyme leaves

1 tablespoon minced fresh sage leaves

1 tablespoon chopped flat-leaf parsley, for garnish

ZINFANDEL GLAZE

1 cup Zinfandel wine

1 red onion, finely chopped

2 cups chicken broth

FOR BALSAMIC MUSHROOM GLAZE

1 Preheat oven to 400°F.

2 Toss the mushrooms with the olive oil, salt, and pepper in a medium bowl. Spread mushrooms in a single layer and roast, turning once, for 7 to 8 minutes, or until soft and browned.

3 Bring the Zinfandel glaze to a simmer over medium heat in a 2-quart saucepan. Add the mushrooms and the balsamic vinegar. Simmer for 10 minutes.

4 Strain the sauce through a fine sieve into a bowl. Sauce can be stored, covered, in the refrigerator, for up to one week.

TO SERVE

Arrange the garlic and herb polenta on 4 warm serving plates. Cut the pork loin crosswise into 20 thick slices and arrange 5 slices on each serving of polenta. Ladle the balsamc mushroom glaze over the pork and top each serving with 5 leaves of fried sage.

2 cups finely chopped mushrooms

2 sprigs fresh thyme

½ teaspoon cracked whole black peppercorns

¼ cup meat trimmings

3 tablespoons all-purpose flour

BALSMAIC MUSHROOM GLAZE

½ pound cremini mushrooms

1 tablespoon olive oil

½ teaspoon coarse salt, or to taste

⅛ teaspoon freshly ground pepper, or to taste

1 cup Zinfandel glaze

3 tablespoons balsamic vinegar

S'MORES GELATO SHAKE

In 2015, Disney Springs became the official name of the shopping, dining, and entertainment area along Village Lake. Set in the heart of the Town Center, D-Luxe Burger is a rustic ranch-inspired restaurant showcasing copper ceiling tiles and a working fireplace. It's also known for delectable gelato shakes.

SERVES 1

MOCKTAIL

12 ounces vanilla gelato

½ ounce dark chocolate sauce

1 ounce toasted marshmallow syrup (can be found at specialty grocers)

1 teaspoon crushed graham crackers

whipped cream, for garnish

mini marshmallows, for garnish

graham cracker, for garnish

dark chocolate sauce, for garnish

Blend vanilla gelato, dark chocolate sauce, toasted marshmallow syrup, and crushed graham crackers until smooth. Serve in tall glass. Garnish with whipped cream, mini marshmallows, graham cracker, and a drizzle of dark chocolate sauce.

D-LUXE BURGER · DISNEY SPRINGS

CHOCOLATE GINGERBREAD SOUFFLÉ WITH CHOCOLATE CREAM SAUCE

Victoria & Albert's is the crème de la crème of Disney dining and has earned numerous prestigious culinary honors, including AAA's illustrious Five Diamond Award. The menu changes daily, but you can master the art of making a sweet light-as-air dessert that is worth remembering. Just be sure to use the freshest ingredients available, and start with egg whites at room temperature. Hot soufflés won't wait; they must be served as soon as they come out of the oven.

MAKES 6-8 SOUFFLÉS   **LEFT THE MENU BUT NOT FORGOTTEN**

GINGERBREAD SOUFFLÉ

6 tablespoons butter, divided

1 ½ cups sugar, divided

9 ounces bittersweet chocolate (60 percent cacao)

2 cups whole milk, divided

¾ cup all-purpose flour

½ teaspoon ground ginger

½ teaspoon ground allspice

½ teaspoon ground cinnamon

¼ teaspoon ground nutmeg

10 egg yolks

10 egg whites

FOR GINGERBREAD SOUFFLÉ

1 Place baking stone or heavy-gauge cookie sheet in oven. Preheat to 375°F.

2 Melt 3 tablespoons butter and brush the insides of six 4½-ounce (or eight 4-ounce) oven-proof ramekins. Coat with ½ cup sugar and shake off excess. Set aside.

3 Melt the chocolate in a heatproof bowl over simmering water. Set aside.

4 Combine ⅓ cup milk with flour, ginger, allspice, cinnamon, and nutmeg in a medium saucepan. Whisk until smooth.

5 Add remaining milk, remaining 3 tablespoons butter, and ½ cup sugar. Bring to a boil, whisking vigorously. Continue to whisk about 5 minutes, until batter pulls away from the sides of the saucepan. Remove from heat and add melted chocolate and egg yolks, mixing until smooth. Set aside.

6 Whip egg whites and remaining ½ cup sugar until stiff peaks form. Fold into chocolate mixture.

7 Fill molds to about ⅛ inch below the rim. Place ramekins on heated baking stone or cookie sheet, allowing several inches between each ramekin. Bake in middle of oven until puffed and crusted on top but still jiggly in center, 18 to 20 minutes.

FOR CHOCOLATE CREAM

1 While soufflé is baking, bring sugar and cream to a boil in a medium saucepan over medium heat. Remove from heat, add chocolate, and whisk until completely melted.

2 Add butter and cognac and whisk continually over low heat just until mixture begins to boil. Remove from heat and keep warm in a double boiler until soufflés are ready to serve.

TO SERVE

Using a spoon, make a split in each soufflé and drizzle warm chocolate sauce. Serve immediately.

CHOCOLATE CREAM

⅓ cup sugar

1 ½ cups heavy cream

9 ounces bittersweet chocolate (60 percent cacao)

1 ½ teaspoons butter

2 teaspoons cognac

NO-BAKE GRANOLA TREATS

What's better than a sweet treat that is a balance of chocolate and peanut butter with hints of crispy bits? How about a *no-bake* treat that's a great recipe for beginner home chefs?

MAKES 12 (2×2-INCH) TREATS **GREAT FOR KIDS**

3½ cups miniature marshmallows

2 tablespoons unsalted butter

3 tablespoons smooth peanut butter

1½ cups granola

¼ cup miniature semisweet chocolate chips

1 In a medium saucepan over low heat, melt marshmallows and butter. Add peanut butter, stirring to combine. Remove from heat. Stir in granola.

2 Spoon mixture into a 6×8-inch baking dish. Lightly press mixture into pan using lightly moistened hands. Sprinkle top of mixture with chocolate chips, lightly pressing the chocolate chips into mixture.

3 Set aside at room temperature to cool for 30 minutes. Cut into 12 pieces. Store treats in an airtight container at room temperature for up to 1 week.

OATMEAL RAISIN COOKIES

Gasparilla Island Grill, near the boat marina of Disney's Grand Floridian Resort & Spa, is a simple but elegant casual dining space, and these crunchy trans fat–free cookies are the ultimate comfort-food treat. The "secret" ingredients: raisins soaked in a little rum, a dollop of thick dark molasses, and crisp granola.

MAKES 1 DOZEN COOKIES

GREAT FOR KIDS

¾ cup raisins

2 tablespoons rum

1 stick of butter, softened

1 teaspoon salt

½ cup sugar

½ cup brown sugar

1 egg

1 ½ teaspoon molasses

1 ¼ cup pastry flour

½ cup all-purpose flour

½ teaspoon baking powder

¾ teaspoon baking soda

1 teaspoon cinnamon

¼ cup granola cereal without raisins

¾ cup oatmeal

1. Preheat oven to 350°F. Lightly grease two cookie sheets

2. Soak raisins in rum in a shallow bowl; set aside.

3. Cream butter, salt, and both sugars with an electric mixer on medium speed. Add the egg and mix thoroughly. Blend in molasses.

4. Add both flours, baking powder, baking soda, cinnamon, granola, and oatmeal and mix thoroughly. Fold in rum-soaked raisins.

5. Drop by heaping tablespoons onto cookie sheets, leaving 2 inches between mounds.

6. Bake for 10 to 12 minutes or until they are a light golden brown.

HONEY CRUNCH CAKE

Like watching a stellar nighttime spectacular from the fifteenth floor viewing deck connected to California Grill, this sweet and crunchy cake is the perfect finale to a fabulous meal.

SERVES 8-12

GREAT FOR KIDS

SPONGE CAKE

½ cup milk

½ cup unsalted butter, cut into pieces

1 ½ cups all-purpose flour

2 teaspoons baking powder

3 large eggs

¼ teaspoon salt

1 cup sugar

¾ teaspoon almond extract

¼ teaspoon vanilla extract

FOR SPONGE CAKE

1 Preheat oven to 375°F. Grease and flour a 9-inch round cake pan.

2 Combine milk and butter in a 1½-quart saucepan and cook over low heat, stirring occasionally, until butter is completely melted. Remove from heat.

3 In a separate bowl, sift together the flour and baking powder. Set aside.

4 In an electric mixer with a whip attachment, mix eggs. Whip in salt, then sugar in a steady stream. Continue to whip for about 30 seconds.

5 Add almond extract and vanilla extract. Gently whip in milk and butter mixture, then gradually add flour mixture, mixing until smooth.

6 Pour batter into prepared 9-inch pan. Bake 20 to 25 minutes, or until the cake is lightly browned and a toothpick inserted in the center comes out clean.

(RECIPE CONTINUES ON PAGE 166)

HONEY CRUNCH CAKE

(CONTINUED)

FOR HONEY CRUNCH

1 Combine water, sugar, and corn syrup in a large saucepan over medium heat. Insert a candy thermometer.

2 When temperature reaches 310°F, whisk in baking soda and turn off heat. Let mixture rise without stirring. Pour onto a nonstick baking mat and completely cool.

3 When cool, break honey crunch into several pieces and store in a resealable plastic bag. Squeeze the bag to break candy into small pieces.

FOR HONEY SIMPLE SYRUP

1 Combine the water and sugar in a saucepan; bring to a boil.

2 Remove from heat and whisk in honey.

3 Store in the refrigerator until ready to use.

FOR HONEY WHIPPED CREAM

1 In an electric mixer with a whip attachment, combine heavy cream and confectioners' sugar. Mix on medium speed for 2 minutes or until cream begins to thicken.

2 Add honey and increase the speed, whipping until medium soft peaks form.

HONEY CRUNCH

3 tablespoons water

1 cup granulated sugar

3 tablespoons corn syrup

2¼ teaspoons baking soda, sifted

HONEY SIMPLE SYRUP

½ cup water

½ cup granulated sugar

2 teaspoons honey

HONEY WHIPPED CREAM

3 cups heavy cream

¾ cup confectioners' sugar

5 tablespoons honey

TO SERVE

1 Cut the cooled cake in half. Reserve top layer.

2 Drizzle the bottom layer with simple syrup.

3 Generously spread whipped cream on the bottom layer, then sprinkle with broken pieces of honey crunch. Spread a little more whipped cream over the honey crunch.

4 Replace the top layer and drizzle with remaining simple syrup.

5 Frost the top and the sides of the cake with remaining whipped cream.

6 Break and arrange remaining honey crunch on each piece. Best when served immediately.

Aulani, A Disney Resort & Spa, 2013

CHAPTER NINE
Beyond the Disney Parks

BLT FLATBREAD

Disney's Vero Beach Resort opened in 1995 on Florida's picturesque Atlantic Treasure Coast. The beachfront resort shares some of its space with the nesting grounds of the loggerhead sea turtle and was thoughtfully designed to allow the turtles to continue their nesting habits uninterrupted by the resort's operations.

From the site's Wind & Waves Grill, this savory flatbread is a great party dish. Just make components ahead of time, then pop in the oven for an easy nosh topped with fresh greens.

MAKES 1 (12-INCH) FLATBREAD   **SAVORY BITES**

GARLIC AIOLI

1 small head fresh garlic

¼ teaspoon olive oil

½ cup mayonnaise

1 tablespoon Dijon mustard

coarse salt, to taste

CARMALIZED ONIONS

1 large onion, thinly sliced

2 tablespoons olive oil

coarse salt, to taste

freshly ground black pepper, to taste

MARINATED TOMATOES

2 medium tomatoes

¼ cup thinly sliced fresh basil

2 teaspoons extra-virgin olive oil

2 teaspoons freshly minced garlic

coarse salt, to taste

freshly ground black pepper, to taste

FOR GARLIC AIOLI

1. Preheat oven to 425°F. Cut top off head of garlic to expose the cloves; drizzle with olive oil and wrap in foil. Roast in preheated oven for an hour, or until garlic is golden brown and very soft. Squeeze garlic out of skins and mash with a fork.

2. Whisk together 2 tablespoons of roasted garlic, mayonnaise, and mustard. Season with salt. Can be made a day ahead and refrigerated.

FOR CARMELIZED ONIONS

1. Combine onions and oil in a large sauté pan. Season with salt and pepper.

2. Cook, stirring often over very low heat, until onions are golden brown and very soft, about 30 minutes. Can be made a day ahead and refrigerated.

FOR MARINATED TOMATOES

1 Cut tomatoes in half and gently squeeze to remove seeds.

2 Dice into ½-inch cubes and stir together in a medium bowl with basil, oil, and garlic. Season with salt and pepper. Can be made a day ahead and refrigerated.

FOR FENNEL-ARUGULA SALAD

1 Cut the top stalks and root end off fennel and discard. Cut fennel in half lengthwise and thinly slice.

2 Coarsely chop arugula and combine with frisée in a large bowl. Toss lettuces with fennel, olive oil, salt, and pepper.

FOR BLT FLATBREADS

1 Preheat oven to 450°F. Place flatbread crust on a baking sheet. Spread with garlic aioli, leaving a ½-inch border around edges. Top with bacon, mozzarella, provolone, and caramelized onions, and finish with marinated tomatoes.

2 Bake 6 to 8 minutes, or until edges are golden brown and cheese is melted. Remove from oven and top with salad. Serve immediately.

FENNEL-ARUGULA SALAD

1 (1-pound) fennel bulb

1 cup fresh arugula

1 cup chopped frisée lettuce

2 teaspoons extra-virgin olive oil

coarse salt and freshly ground black pepper, to taste

BLT FLATBREAD

12-inch prepared flatbread

1 cup chopped cooked bacon

½ cup shredded mozzarella cheese

½ cup shredded provolone cheese

TUNA POKE WITH AVOCADO MOUSSE

Aulani, A Disney Resort & Spa opened in 2011 on twenty-one acres in Ko Olina Resort & Marina on the Hawaiian island of Oahu. It includes eight eateries across the resort, ranging from quick-service spots to fine dining. The resort's chefs prepare dishes inspired by the island's local delicacies, including this take on poke.

SERVES 6 AS AN APPETIZER   **SAVORY BITES**

FOR TUNA POKE

1. Whisk together soy sauce, ginger, sesame oil, yuzu juice, lime juice, garlic, sesame seeds, vinegar, wasabi powder, and sugar in a large bowl.

2. Add tuna to mixture and toss to coat. Season with pepper, to taste. Refrigerate 5 to 10 minutes.

FOR AVOCADO MOUSSE

1. Chop avocados into large pieces and place in a blender. Add heavy cream and blend until smooth.

2. Season with lime juice, salt, and white pepper, to taste.

TUNA POKE

1 cup soy sauce

2 tablespoons freshly grated ginger

2 tablespoons sesame oil

2 tablespoons yuzu juice

juice of 1 lime

1 tablespoon finely minced garlic

1 tablespoon toasted sesame seeds, plus additional for garnish

1 tablespoon rice vinegar

1 teaspoon wasabi powder

1/8 teaspoon sugar

2 pounds fresh sushi-grade tuna, cubed

freshly ground black pepper, to taste

AVOCADO MOUSSE

2 ripe avocados, peeled and pitted

2 tablespoons heavy cream

lime juice

salt, to taste

white pepper, to taste

TO SERVE

1 Place avocado mousse in a piping bag. Pipe 3 parallel lines of avocado mousse in the center of each plate.

2 Divide tuna poke evenly among six 2½-inch square molds. Place on top of the avocado mousse.

3 Serve with rice chips.

GARNISH

rice chips

POG BREAKFAST JUICE

A Hawaiian breakfast would not be complete without Disney's spin on the iconic POG juice blend!

MAKES 12 CUPS

MOCKTAIL

4 cups passion fruit juice

4 cups orange juice

4 cups guava juice

Mix all ingredients together in a 1-gallon pitcher. Serve over ice in a tall glass.

CASTAWAY WAVE

The name of this beverage recalls the name of Castaway Cay. A one-thousand-acre uninhabited island in The Bahamas originally known as Gorda Cay, Castaway Cay was purchased and renamed by Disney in 1996. Since then it has been used as a daylong recreation stopover for Disney Cruise Line ships in the area.

- 1 ounce coconut rum
- ½ ounce apple pucker
- ½ ounce Midori
- 1 ½ ounces pineapple juice

SERVES 1

COCKTAIL

In a cocktail shaker, mix all ingredients together. Serve in a cocktail glass over ice.

BLUE HAWAIIAN

'Ōlelo (pronounced oh-leh-low) is a Hawaiian word meaning "conversing" and inspired the 'Ōlelo Room, a lounge that honors Hawaiian language through its cultural-heritage stories, décor, and even pronunciation guidance from its bartenders. Naturally, this spot also offers the Disney spin on recognizable Hawaiian fruit drinks.

To re-create the house-made sweet and sour, combine 2 parts citrus juice (for example, a squeeze of lemon, lime, or orange) with 1 part granulated sugar and 1 part water.

1 ounce house-made sweet and sour

2 ounces pineapple juice

1 ounce light rum, Old Lahaina preferred

1 ounce vodka, Ocean preferred

½ ounce blue curaçao, BOLS preferred

Pineapple wedge and pineapple leaf, for garnish

SERVES 1

COCKTAIL

1 Pour sweet and sour, pineapple juice, rum, and blue curaçao into mixing glass. Fill with ice and shake for 30 seconds.

2 Pour into tall glass; garnish with pineapple wedge and pineapple leaf.

"COLETTE" CHAMPAGNE COCKTAIL

Remy is the most luxurious dinner experience on board the *Disney Dream* and *Disney Fantasy* sh ps. Elegantly drawing inspiration from *Ratatouille* (2007), this French restaurant is an adult-exclusive venue. This cocktail takes inspiration from Colette, the film's experienced chef at Gusteau's who is tasked with teaching rookie chef Linguini the basics of cooking.

SERVES 1

COCKTAIL

3 crème de cassis pearls

½ ounce orange-flavored liqueur

½ ounce vodka

4 ounces Champagne

2 dried pineapple cubes

1 Place crème de cassis pearls in bottom of martini g ass.

2 Add orange-flavored liqueur, followed by vodka. Top with Champagne.

3 Finish with dried pineapple cubes.

BELOW, LEFT: The *Disney Fantasy* cruise ship docked at Castaway Cay, 2017

PADDY MINT MOCHA

This specialty coffee, served during the winter holidays on the Disney Cruise Line ships, is a festive ending for a dinner party.

SERVES 1

MOCKTAIL

1 ounce espresso

1 ounce chocolate mint syrup

2 ounces chocolate syrup, divided

11 ounces steamed milk

whipped cream, for topping

sprig of mint, for garnish

1 Mix espresso, chocolate mint syrup, and 1 ounce of chocolate syrup in a glass mug. Slowly pour in warm milk. Top with whipped cream and drizzle with remaining chocolate syrup.

2 Garnish with a sprig of mint, if desired.

KONK KOOLER

SWEET ENDINGS AND DESSERTS

This frozen concoction of light and dark rum is a signature drink on Castaway Cay, Disney's private island in The Bahamas, a stop on every Disney Cruise Line ship's itinerary.

SERVES 1　　　　　　　　　　　　　　**COCKTAIL**

½ ounce dark rum

¾ ounce light rum

1 ounce passion fruit juice

1 ounce piña colada mix

1 ounce orange juice

crushed ice

cherry, for garnish

1　Place the first five ingredients in a cocktail shaker and shake vigorously.

2　Serve in a tall glass filled with crushed ice. Garnish with a cherry, if desired.

COCONUT CREAM FRENCH MACARONS

Located on the beautiful beaches of the leeward coast of Oahu, Hawaii, Aulani, A Disney Resort & Spa, welcomes guests from all over the world. These coconut cream macarons offer a taste of the islands with a French flair.

MAKES 12 MACARONS **LEFT THE MENU BUT NOT FORGOTTEN**

MACARONS

¾ cup almond flour

1 ¼ cups powdered sugar, divided

2 egg whites

1 pinch cream of tartar

FOR MACARONS

1 Preheat oven to 350°F. Line a baking sheet with a nonstick silicone mat or parchment paper; set aside.

2 Pulse almond flour and 1 cup powdered sugar in a food processor until combined. Sift twice, discarding larger pieces. Set aside.

3 Combine egg whites, remaining ¼ cup powdered sugar, and cream of tartar in the bowl of an electric mixer fitted with a whisk attachment. Beat on low speed until mixture is combined, then increase speed to high and beat until mixture is thick and glossy and holds stiff peaks, 7 to 8 minutes.

4 Sift almond flour mixture into beaten egg-white mixture. Gently fold until batter is smooth and shiny and drips slowly away when spatula is lifted. Transfer batter to a pastry bag fitted with a ½-inch round tip. Pipe ¾-inch rounds onto a prepared baking sheet, spacing 1 inch apart. Lightly tap baking sheet against countertop to release any air bubbles. Set aside at room temperature 15 to 20 minutes. (This allows the top of the macaron to form a crust so that when it bakes, a smooth top is formed.)

5 Bake 10 to 12 minutes, or until macarons are firm but not brown. Let cool on baking sheet 2 to 3 minutes, then transfer to a wire rack to cool completely.

FOR COCONUT CREAM FILLING

1 Combine coconut milk, sugar, and cornstarch in a small saucepan over medium-high heat, bring to a boil, whisking continuously until mixture thickens.

2 Transfer to a medium bowl. Cover with plastic wrap, pressing wrap directly onto surface of mixture. Set aside to cool to room temperature, then refrigerate until cool.

3 Whisk in butter and powdered sugar until slightly fluffy and smooth. Spoon into a piping bag fitted with a small round tip.

4 Lay half the macarons out on a work surface, flat side up. Pipe a small amount of coconut cream filling onto each macaron. Top with remaining macarons, creating 12 sandwiches.

COCONUT CREAM FILLING

⅓ cup coconut milk

2 tablespoons sugar

1 tablespoon cornstarch

⅓ cup unsalted butter, softened

3 tablespoons powdered sugar

CARAMEL HAWAIIAN SWEET BREAD PUDDING

Fluffy Hawaiian sweet bread was created in Hawaii in the 1950s and remains a quintessential taste of the islands. This sweet bread pudding is a favorite on the buffet at Makahiki—The Bounty of the Islands restaurant. The interior of Makahiki showcases beautiful works by local artists, from paintings to glass art.

SERVES 8

A DISNEY CLASSIC

- 5 cups 1-inch-cubed Hawaiian sweet bread
- 1½ cups sugar, divided
- ⅓ cup water
- 6 eggs
- 3 cups whole milk
- 2 teaspoons vanilla extract
- 1 pinch salt
- 1 teaspoon ground cinnamon

1. Preheat oven to 250°F. Place bread cubes in an even layer on two sheet pans. Toast bread until it feels dry and is light golden, about 15 to 25 minutes. Set aside.

2. Combine 1 cup sugar and water in a medium saucepan over medium heat, stirring until sugar dissolves.

3. Raise heat to medium-high and cook without stirring or touching pan until liquid caramelizes and turns dark gold.

4. Pour caramel into a 9-inch-square baking dish, tilting dish slightly in all directions to allow caramel to coat bottom surface. Set aside.

5. Increase oven temperature to 350°F.

6. Whisk eggs and remaining ½ cup sugar together until just combined. Whisk in milk, vanilla extract, and salt until well combined and sugar dissolves. Pour mixture through a fine-mesh sieve. Set aside.

7 Fill prepared dish with toasted bread; pour ¾ of custard mixture over toasted bread. Press bread down with the back of a large spoon. Pour remaining custard mixture over bread. Press down again with the spoon, allowing bread to soak up liquid.

8 Sprinkle cinnamon evenly over top. Wrap pan in aluminum foil.

9 Slide center rack out of oven; place dish inside a larger baking pan on center rack. Fill larger pan with water until it reaches halfway up sides of baking dish.

10 Carefully slide center rack into oven. Bake until set and a small knife inserted into the center comes out clean, about 1 hour and 15 minutes.

11 Uncover dish and set aside to cool in water 20 minutes; run a paring knife along sides of bread pudding to loosen. Carefully invert onto serving platter and serve warm.

ORANGE ALMOND CAKE WITH LEMON CREAM

This elegantly simple gluten-free dessert is a big hit at Palo on the Disney Cruise Line ships. They serve it with an orange fennel salad and rhubarb puree, but this at-home version highlights the flavors of the cake and rich lemon cream.

SERVES 12

A DISNEY CLASSIC

ORANGE ALMOND CAKE

2½ cups almond flour

1 teaspoon baking powder

6 eggs, separated

1¾ cups sugar

⅓ cup orange juice

2 tablespoons lemon juice

2 teaspoons orange zest

FOR ORANGE ALMOND CAKE

1 Preheat oven to 325°F. Grease an 8-inch-square baking dish with nonstick cooking spray.

2 Sift together almond flour and baking powder; set aside.

3 Whip egg whites in bowl of electric mixer on high until soft peaks form. Set aside.

4 Mix sugar and egg yolks in bowl of an electric mixer on medium speed until light and fluffy, about 2 minutes. Reduce to low speed and add orange juice.

5 Slowly add almond flour and baking powder with mixer on low speed. Add lemon juice and orange zest; mix on low speed for 1 minute.

6 Fold in a small amount of egg whites until fully mixed. Gently fold in remaining egg white. Mixture should be light and fluffy.

7 Spread in prepared baking dish. Bake for 40 to 45 minutes, or until a toothpick inserted in the center comes out clean. Cool at least 2 hours before frosting.

FOR LEMON CREAM

1 Mix ingredients in a medium bowl for 2 minutes, until well blended and thickened.

2 Spread a thin layer over cooled cake.

LEMON CREAM

¼ cup heavy cream

⅔ cups mascarpone cheese

¼ lemon, juiced and zested

½ cup powdered sugar

ACKNOWLEDGMENTS

Jennifer Eastwood and team get full credit for imagining this fun book that showcases our incredible chefs, and my sincere thanks to Lindsay Broderick for artistically bringing it all together. I was fortunate to work with a core team on many of the Disney cookbooks, and their creativity shines in this best-of collection: Karen McClintock, Matt Stroshane, James Kilby, Jason Farmand, Katie Farmand, Katie Wilson, Jessie Ward, Michele Gendreau, Stacy Malone, Karlos Siqueiros, and David Nguyen. And most of all, thanks to the Disney chefs around the globe for sharing their secrets.

—Pam Brandon

THIS BOOK'S PRODUCERS WOULD LIKE TO SPECIALLY THANK Nicole Carroll, Jonathan Chew, Becky Cline, Alyce Diamandis, Jeffrey R. Epstein, Debra Kohls, Aileen Kutaka, Mark LaVine, Karen McClintock, Courtney McIntyre, Michael Mendez, Matt Moryc, Chris Ostrander, Diego Parras, Frank Reifsnyder, David Roark, Carmen Smith, Dave Stern, Matt Stroshane, Kimi Thompson, Janice Thomson, Steven Vagnini, Cayla Ward, and Juleen Woods.

ALSO THANK YOU TO THOSE AT DISNEY PUBLISHING: Jennifer Black, Lori Campos, Max Calne, Rob Celauro, Ann Day, Monique Diman, Jim Fanning, Michael Freeman, Alison Giordano, Daneen Goodwin, Maureen Graham, Tyra Harris, Winnie Ho, Molly Jones, Jackson Kaplan, Kim Knueppel, Vicki Korlishin, Kaitie Leary, Renee Leask, Meredith Lisbin, Warren Meislin, Lia Murphy, Scott Piehl, Dominique Pietz, Mariel Pinciotti, Tim Retzlaff, Rachel Rivera, Carol Roeder, Julie Rose, Danny Saeva, Andrew Sansone, Zan Schneider, Alexandra Serrano, Fanny Sheffield, Dina Sherman, Ken Shue, Marina Shults, Annie Skogsbergh, Megan Speer-Levi, Jenny Spring, Muriel Tebid, Pat Van Note, Lynn Waggoner, Jessie Ward, and Rudy Zamora.

INDEX

Index of Recipe Sources

BIBLIOGRAPHY & SOURCES

BOOKS

Brandon, Pam, and Marcy Carriker Smothers and the Disney Chefs. *Delicious Disney: Walt Disney World: Recipes & Stories from The Most Magical Place on Earth*. Los Angeles • New York: Disney Editions, 2021.

Brandon, Pam and the Disney Chefs. *Delicious Disney: The Fresh Edition*. Los Angeles • New York: Disney Editions, 2019.

—. *Disney Festivals Cookbook: 50 New Recipes, 6 Fabulous Festivals*. Lake Buena Vista, Florida • Anaheim, Californian: The Walt Disney Company, 2018.

—. *Delicious Disney: Sweet Treats*. Los Angeles • New York: Disney Editions, 2016.

—. *EPCOT International Food & Wine Festival: Recipes & Stories Celebrating 20 Years*. Lake Buena Vista, Florida • Anaheim, Californian: The Walt Disney Company, 2015.

—. *A Cooking Safari with Mickey*. Los Angeles • New York: Disney Editions, 2015.

—. *Kitchen Magic with Mickey*. Los Angeles • New York: Disney Editions, 2014.

—. *Delicious Disney: Great for Kids*. New York: Disney Editions, 2011.

—. *Chef Mickey*. New York: Disney Editions, 2010.

—. *Delicious Disney: Desserts*. New York: Disney Editions, 2008.

—. *Delicious Disney*. New York: Disney Editions, 2006.

—. *Cooking with Mickey and the Disney Chefs*. New York: Disney Editions, 2004.

—. *Cooking with Mickey and the Chefs of Walt Disney World Resort*. New York: Hyperion, 1998.

Disney Chefs. *Cooking with Mickey around Our World: The MOST Requested Recipes from Walt Disney World and Disneyland*. Lake Buena Vista, Florida • Anaheim, Californian: The Walt Disney Company, 1986.

—. *Mickey's Gourmet Cookbook: The Most Popular Recipes from Walt Disney World and Disneyland*. New York: Hyperion, 1994.

—. *Mickey's Gourmet Cookbook—Cooking with Mickey, Volume II: The Most Requested Recipes from Walt Disney World and Disneyland*. New York: Hyperion, 1999

IMAGE CREDITS

BRING HOME THE TASTE OF THE
DISNEY PARKS